CENTURY OF THE DEATH OF THE ROSE

CENTURY
OF THE
DEATH
OF THE
ROSE
SELECTED POEMS

JORGE CARRERA ANDRADE

EDITED AND TRANSLATED BY
STEVEN FORD BROWN

NEWSOUTH BOOKS
Montgomery

NewSouth Books
P.O. Box 1588
Montgomery, AL 36102

ISBN 1-58838-102-1

Design by Randall Williams
Printed in the United States of America

Front cover art: "Cattleya Orchid and Three Brazilian Hummingbirds" by Martin Johnson Heade, 1871, oil on wood, Gift of the Morris and Cafritz Foundation, Photograph courtesy of and © Board of Trustees, National Gallery of Art, Washington, DC.

ABOUT THE ARTIST

Martin Johnson Heade, a member of the Hudson River School of painting, was born in 1819 and reared in Lumberville, a small rural community near Doylestown, in Buck's County, Pennsylvania. Primarily a self-taught artist with no formal training, he took a study trip in 1840 to Europe where he spent two years in Rome. From then on Heade was a constant traveler, never stopping anywhere long enough to put down roots. By turn he lived in New York, Philadelphia, Rome again, Saint Louis, Chicago, Trenton, Providence, Boston, and St. Augustine, Florida.

Influenced by landscape painters, particularly Frederic Edwin Church, the period after 1863 marks the maturing of his personal style of landscape painting. Critics invariably refer to his interest in the broad panoramas of landscapes, subtle atmospheric effects, the detailed preciseness of his renderings of the natural world, and his attempts to capture the fleeting beauty of nature. Beginning in 1863 Heade took several trips to Brazil to begin painting a complete series of South American hummingbirds and orchids. His later years were devoted to floral still lifes, recurring scenes from the South American landscapes of his travels, and the coastal landscapes of New England, for which he is most often remembered today.

Although Heade exhibited widely—at the National Academy of Design, the Pennsylvania Academy of the Fine Arts, the American Art-Union, the Boston Athenaeum, and Royal Academy in London—he did not achieve noticeable recognition during his lifetime. His paintings were rediscovered during a 1940s revival of interest in the Hudson River School of painting and are today considered to be the work of a premier American artist.

FOR J. ENRIQUE OJEDA

Contents

IV. Boletines de Viaje / Traveler's Bulletins

Appendix

Acknowledgments

I am indebted to the editors of the following literary journals where these translations were first published:

The Antioch Review, "Sum"; *The Atlanta Review*, "Evening Edition" and "The Terrestrians"; *Chelsea*, "The Number," "The Object and Its Shadow," and "The Whole Image"; *The Georgetown Review*, "The World's Breakfast"; *Green Mountains Review*, "Nameless Region" and "Time's Workshop"; *Hayden's Ferry Review*, "Hydrographic Poem"; *The Literary Review*, "October"; *The Marlboro Review*, "Bad Humor" and "Loneliness of Cities"; *Nimrod*, "April" and "God of Joy"; *Poet Lore*, "Weathervane on the Cathedral"; *Quarterly West*, "A Dream of Farmhouses" and "Traveler's Bulletin"; *Verse*, "Biography," "Contemporary History," "Movements of Nature," and "The Parachutist's Notebook."

"Biography for the Use of Birds" and "Sunday" first appeared in *Poetry*. Copyright 1998 by the Modern Poetry Association. Reprinted with permission of *Poetry*.

Various translations of Jorge Carrera Andrade have also appeared in online literary journals.

The United States:

"Biography for the Use of Birds" is included in a brief biographical profile of Jorge Carrera Andrade at *Britannica.com*.

My appreciation to Guy Sahar of *The Cortland Review* for publishing "The Clock," "Song of the Apple," and "Spring & Co."

Rebecca Seiferle published the following poems in a special feature on the poetry of Jorge Carrera Andrade in *The Drunken Boat*: "Election

Handbill for Green," "Festival of San Pedro," "Hydrographic Poem," "Sierra," and "Sunday."

Sydney, Australia:

John Tratner was kind enough to publish a special profile on the poetry and life of Jorge Carrera Andrade in Jacket, including an early version of the introduction and the following poems: "Anonymous Speech," "Biography," "Biography for the Use of Birds," "A Dream of Farmhouses," "Ecuadorian Man Under the Eiffel Tower," "Indian Rebellion," "Loneliness of Cities," "Nothing," "Power of the Word," "The Return Journey," "Portrait of Man," and "Sunday."

The chronology of Jorge Carrera Andrade's life is by J. Enrique Ojeda from the Spanish edition of *El volcán y el colibrí*, an autobiography by Jorge Carrera Andrade, Corporacion Editora Nacional, Quito, 1989.

Translator's Notes

The completed manuscript of *Century of the Death of the Rose* has been the result of a series of happy accidents. At an idle point in my life I discovered a single poem by Jorge Carrera Andrade in a now-forgotten anthology of world poets. In love with his work but dissatisfied with the quality of the translation, I began translating his poetry for pleasure.

After a summer of leisurely translating I was pleasantly surprised to discover that some sixty poems had been completed. I then began thinking seriously about book publication. Various attempts to locate the Carrera Andrade family through diplomatic and governmental avenues in Washington, D.C. (he was a former diplomat), for permission to translate and publish were futile. A diplomatic contact in El Salvador eventually passed on the name of the Cultural Attaché at the U.S. Embassy in Quito, Terry R. Davidson, who as it turns out had once worked for *The Boston Globe*.

Mr. Davidson communicated several weeks later that the authoritative international expert on the poetry and life of Jorge Carrera Andrade was Professor J. Enrique Ojeda of Boston College, an Ecuadorian whose Ph.D. dissertation at Harvard University thirty years earlier had been on the poetry of Carrera Andrade. In the intervening years Ojeda had also published a critical book, *Jorge Carrera Andrade: Introducción al estudio de su vida y de su obra* (1972).

In the summer of 1998, I traveled to Wellesley, Massachusetts, to Ojeda's home to view his collection of Carrera Andrade books, papers, and photographs. We continued meeting for the next several years over dinners at various Boston and Wellesley cafes and restaurants, discussing the life and work of what came to be known between us as "our poet."

Our close and unique collaboration to promote the work and life of Jorge Carrera Andrade has turned into a lasting friendship.

I should also note that Dr. Ojeda has been the intellectual compass that has guided me in navigating my way through the intricacies of South American history and the various movements of literary modernism. His corrections and suggestions during the proofreading stage of the manuscript have been essential in creating the best possible representation of the life and work of "our poet" Jorge Carrera Andrade.

Over the past four years other friends have drifted in and out of the picture to provide various forms of assistance with this project: Juan Carrera Colin, Quito, Ecuador, granted permission to translate the poetry of his father; my long-time friends Richard Peabody, Jan Susina, and Nicomedes Suarez-Arauz read and commented on early drafts of the manuscript; Jim Shakin and Ingrid Geis have continued to be supportive of my work; Yim Tan Lisa Wong's enthusiasm for this project has been a source of sustenance; Victoria A. Slingerland provided a close and inspirational reading of the draft manuscript, and her suggestions for revision were, in several instances, crucial in the final shaping of the manuscript. I should also extend my appreciation to the Special Collection libraries of SUNY Stony Brook (Jorge Carrera Andrade Collection), University of Delaware (John Malcolm Brinnin Collection), and Princeton University (John Peale Bishop Collection) for assistance in locating and obtaining copies of correspondence, documents and manuscripts for my research.

—SFB

An Introduction
to Jorge Carrera Andrade

OF CELESTIAL NAVIGATIONS

At the close of the twentieth century, the skies over the central and southern parts of the continent of the Americas were crisscrossed with the residual lights of flashing comets and stars of poets that emerged during the era: the extravagant light of Rubén Darío; the powerful masculine-feminine sun of Pablo Neruda; the searing human starlight of César Vallejo; sparks given off by the flint and stone creationist poetics of Vicente Huidobro; and the infinite indigenous light of Octavio Paz. All of these poets left their celestial marks on the heavens.

Each of these poets was important to the theory and execution of the new modern and post-modern Portuguese and Spanish language poetry of the hemisphere. The celestial metaphor may seem fantastical and yet it is fitting for a land that has always been imbued with more myth than reality. Indeed, everything about the countries the Spanish discovered and then fought for—as often against each other as the indigenous peoples—was fantastic: tangled and secretive jungles, vast rivers and towering mountains, erupting volcanoes, sophisticated native cities and cultures, and the legends of real and imagined treasures.

But there was another poet in South American literature during this era, a luminous presence that hovered over the landscape near the horizon. His name was Jorge Carrera Andrade, an Ecuadorian, who spent his entire adult life traveling as a diplomat and poet. Yet despite a brief flurry of attention generated by his book, *Secret Country* (New York: MacMillan, 1946), published just after he served as Ecuadorian Consul

General in San Francisco, Jorge Carrera Andrade has since been forgotten by anthologists and literary critics in the United States.

DARÍO AND THE ORNAMENTATION OF THE LITERARY LANDSCAPE

Even after the British (and stormy seas) sank the "invincible" armada of Phillip II in 1588, Spain continued to dominate the search for new lands and the carving out of lucrative footholds in the New World. Legend holds that the silver mines of Potosi in Bolivia alone yielded enough silver in those early colonial centuries to build a bridge across the Atlantic from Spanish America to Spain. But after the defeat of Spanish forces and liberation of the southern continent by José de San Martín and Simón Bolívar at Ayacucho in Perú on December 9, 1824, the inevitable diminishment of Spain as a world power was confirmed by its defeat at the hands of the United States during the Spanish American War of 1898.

Like the volcanoes that shook the earth of the central and southern parts of the continent, Nicaraguan poet Rubén Darío erupted on the literary scene in 1888 with the publication of his book of poems and stories, *Azul*. Darío was a cosmopolitan dandy and international traveler who shook the dust from the pages of a Spanish American literature that had reached a dead end. Darío's embrace of the modernist impulse emanating from Europe allowed him to tear away the musty romantic clothing of the old continental literature and put on the new suit of Symbolism fashioned from French cloth. As English Romanticism declined on the European continent and French Symbolism flourished, Darío embraced the new and spread the word in his travels throughout the cultural capitals of Spanish America about new possibilities for literature. The day of Symbolism passed quickly within three decades and new generations of writers arose to throw off the ornamentation of Darío and the Symbolists. With the arrival of the new century and ideas generated by modernism and the other movements of the era—Cubism, Futurism, Surrealism, Ultraism—there were the inevitable concerns writers had about the evolution of their writing. Spanish American writers began to wrestle with a variety of questions and themes: the advent of World War I and growing development of their own cultural and financial capitals, which had the residual effect of sowing the internal seeds of nationalism; the break with a Spain humiliated by its defeat in the War of 1898; and a look back over their shoulders in the mirror at their own indigenous reflections.

THE ORIGINS OF JORGE CARRERA ANDRADE

From a prominent family—his father was a member of the Ecuadorian Supreme Court and his mother the daughter of an army general—Jorge Carrera Andrade grew up in Quito. During his childhood on the family's country estate, he developed sympathetic relationships with the Indians who worked the land. His father's views from the judicial bench—very liberal for this era in Spanish America—were also sympathetic to the plight of the Indians. Within a short time after graduation from high school, Carrera Andrade was quickly involved in both local and national politics. While still in his early thirties, he was appointed a diplomat to France. For the next four decades, he would hold a variety of diplomatic postings (Japan, the Netherlands, Nicaragua, Venezuela, the United Kingdom, and the United States), and positions at the United Nations and UNESCO.

Even as a beginning writer Jorge Carrera Andrade's first poems were ambitious and polished. With Francis Jammes as an early influence, he experimented with a variety of styles and forms. Upon departing for Europe in his late twenties, Carrera Andrade became, like many artists before him, a student in the university of European ideas. In Paris and Spain he met and associated with numerous fellow South American expatriates, including Gabriela Mistral and César Vallejo.

Following up on his encounters with Ultraism in Ecuador from his friendship with César Arroyo, he continued in Europe to experiment with the ideas of Cansinos Assens and Guillermo de Torre. Assens and de Torre formulated Ultraism in Madrid as a poetic that utilized the metaphor as a primary compositional tool. Although Carrera Andrade embraced Ultraism for a brief period, it has been pointed out by H. R. Hays that he was never a true Ultraist. Hays notes that Carrera Andrade's images were never the product of naiveté or neosurrealism. He was more the scientist in a laboratory mixing, experimenting, and theorizing until he was able to successfully marry his poetic metaphor with the natural surroundings of his native Ecuador.

In his best work from the 1920s and 1930s, the poems are portraits of simple objects and landscapes, most often the Indians and their villages. The visual images he created in the early poems are so striking his poetry from that period is the equivalent of visual painting with words. The intense clarity of his images obscures the brush strokes and the result is the addition of another dimension to the poem. Whereas most poems are clearly flat or two-dimensional on the page, the most accomplished of Carrera Andrade's poems adds a third dimension so the images are endowed with the luster and pulse of light, the contemporary feel of life. Although an example of this technique often cited is the poem "Sierra," with its visual image of corn hanging by its husks from roof beams of the Indian hut—"Ears of corn, with canary wings,/hung from roof beams."— a more powerful and unusual example is from "Dining Room Mirror":

>The dining room mirror
>builds squares and
>figures of incandescent geometry.
>
>It hoists wavering planes
>to its blue level.
>It measures objects
>with compasses of light.
>
>It shuffles certainties.
>Fences diameters.
>Threads lights.
>
>Its crystal ruler breaks
>the nude water bottle
>and a slanting stream of diamonds

flows toward the dark table.

In "Hydrographic Poem," the poet looks at a map of the world and sees the story, the biographies of rivers:

> Rivers seek each other throughout the world,
> and spread throughout the earth their glass trumpets.
> Navigation charts collect
> the blue biographies of rivers.

William Carlos Williams in a letter to Muna Lee, the translator of *Secret Country*, remarks that Carrera Andrade's images are so remarkably clear, the poems are "freed from the torment of the mind which has become our daily bread."

TRAVELER OF VISTAS AND COUNTRIES

After his initial posting in France, Jorge Carrera Andrade rose quickly through the Ecuadorian diplomatic ranks. He became then a man constantly on the move. In December of 1940 Jorge Carrera Andrade stepped ashore at the port of San Francisco, California. Appointed as Ecuadorian Consul General, Carrera Andrade had just spent two and a half years in Japan as its military forces began their sweep through Asia and Indochina. In that same period Belgium, France, Luxembourg, the Netherlands, Norway, and Poland had fallen to the Germans. In December of 1940 the Luftwaffe had begun its bombing campaign of Britain. The entry of the United States into the global war was inevitable.

Carrera Andrade's first period in the United States was to last four years. As he had always done in whatever city he was posted to, Carrera Andrade continued his active literary life. In California he met and became close friends with Spanish poet in exile Pedro Salinas. He also engaged in extensive literary correspondences with many U.S. writers, including John Peale Bishop, Dudley Fitts, H. R. Hays, John Hersey, Muna Lee, James Laughlin, Seymour Lawrence, Thomas Merton,

Archibald MacLeish, Wallace Stevens, Donald Walsh, and William Carlos Williams. His international correspondents around the same time included Jaime Torres Bodet, Eugenio Florit, Yvan Goll, Jorge Guillén, Nicolás Guillén, Juan Liscano, Gabriela Mistral, Pablo Neruda, Carlos Pellicer, Edouard Roditi, and Jules Supervielle.

In 1942 James Laughlin's New Directions Publishers published a massive anthology of South American poets. Under the editorship of Dudley Fitts, with the logistical assistance of Carrera Andrade, the anthology weighed in at more than five hundred pages and was the first comprehensive anthology of South American poets to be published in English. In its pages readers gained their first significant glimpses of, among others, Carrera Andrade, Miguel Angel Asturias, Jorge Luis Borges, Pablo Antonio Cuadra, Carlos Drummond de Andrade, Vicente Huidobro, Gabriela Mistral, Pablo Neruda, and César Vallejo.

By 1943 essays by and about Jorge Carrera Andrade were beginning to appear in the major American literary journals of the time. H. R. Hays wrote and published an eloquent appraisal, "Jorge Carrera Andrade: Magician of Metaphors," as the lead feature of the distinguished international literary journal *Books Abroad* (now *World Literature Today*) at the University of Oklahoma. *Poetry* magazine in Chicago published a major essay by Carrera Andrade (translated from the Spanish by Hays). Although fifty years later the essay, "The New American and His Point of View Toward Poetry," is dated, at the time of publication it was a dazzling survey of the contemporary South American poetry scene of the 1940s, a series of snapshots of an exciting and evolving literary scene from the inside.

By the time the essay appeared in 1943 the United States was fully engaged in World War II in both Europe and the Pacific. Carrera Andrade's portrait of the poetry of the central and southern continent of the Americas and the Caribbean was both poetic and evocative. It's clear he envisioned a future poetry that would combine all the elements of the hemisphere to allow the new American to speak with the voice of the changing century. For many U.S. readers it was an eloquent introduction to a new literature emerging from European models to maturity as a purely South American literature. Carrera Andrade also used the essay to draw attention to the fact that a number of South American countries were contributing their sons to the fight for democratic ideals in Europe. In the same breath in which he promoted South American literature and culture, he was aware of the need to lobby for political support for the countries south of the United States borders.

The appearance of the essay in *Poetry* immediately drew letters from Wallace Stevens and William Carlos Williams. Williams wrote from his New Jersey home to the editor of *Poetry* that " . . . if the essay had appeared twenty years earlier it would have saved us all a great deal of work." Stevens, in a handwritten letter on the letterhead of the Hartford Life Insurance Company, noted that he was impressed by the essay and invited Carrera Andrade to meet with him in New York.

In 1944 Carrera Andrade was appointed ambassador to Venezuela and left the United States. In 1946 the publication of his first major book in English, *Secret Country* (New York: MacMillan, 1946), translated by Muna Lee, wife of the then governor of Puerto Rico, drew praise in the pages of *The Chicago Times, Hispania, The New York Times, The New Yorker, The Partisan Review, Saturday Review of Literature,* and *The Yale Review.* Carl Sandburg, writing in Spanish from his farm in Flat Rock, North Carolina, sent a letter to Lee praising the poetry of Carrera Andrade, calling him his "brother in the poetry quest."

Within the next ten years additional essays, articles, and reviews of his work would appear in the United States, England, France, Belgium, and the Netherlands. From 1952–58, Carrera Andrade lived in Paris and worked at UNESCO. He continued his literary activities there, including two books published in bilingual Spanish-French editions. Although Carrera Andrade made short trips to the United States as part of his duties with UNESCO or as a delegate to the United Nations, it was not until 1968–71 that he spent another substantial period in the U.S.

During the intervening years a number of other translations of his work appeared. *Visitor of Mist,* a book of poetry translated by G. R. Coulthard, was published in England in 1950. J. M. Cohen included Carrera Andrade in his *Penguin Book of Spanish Verse* (England, 1956) and Willis Barnstone included his poetry in *Modern European Poetry*

(New York, 1966). Carrera Andrade also appeared in Danish, French, and German anthologies. Thomas Merton, John Malcolm Brinnin, and Donald Walsh translated various poems for anthologies, books, and magazines. While Brinnin's translations on the whole are unaccomplished, Thomas Merton managed to capture the flavor and delicacy of Carrera Andrade's poems in a small collection of translations he included in *Emblems of a Season of Fury* (1963), one of Merton's many books of poetry from New Directions. Usually an excellent translator and editor, H. R. Hays published a flawed and poorly edited book, *Selected Poems*, in 1972 with SUNY Press. An even worse rendering of Jorge Carrera Andrade came with the SUNY Press publication in English of a collection of his lectures, *Reflections on Latin American Literature* (1973).

From 1969–71, Carrera Andrade taught at SUNY Stony Brook while living on Long Island. He traveled to give lectures at Harvard University and Vassar College and also participated in a poetry gathering at Lincoln Center in New York City. Attendees at the Lincoln Center event included Carrera Andrade, John Malcolm Brinnin, Jim Harrison, Anthony Hecht, Zbigniew Herbert, Czeslaw Milosz, John Logan, J. Enrique Ojeda, Nicanor Parra, Henry Rago, Louis Simpson, William Jay Smith, and James Tate. Soon after, Carrera Andrade also participated in a poetry festival and recorded his poems in Spanish at the Library of Congress.

At the age of seventy, as he mentions in his Vassar College lecture, Jorge Carrera Andrade had come full circle. Throughout his life and career he was a man constantly on the move. He was a diplomat posted to a variety of countries, often sent to negotiate or lobby for Ecuador's financial or political needs. He was hired and fired, reassigned, or sought other employment according to the political winds that blew through the presidential palace. He spent his last years in Quito with a modest stipend as Director of the National Library.

Since his death in 1978 Jorge Carrera Andrade has suffered a decline in his literary reputation in the United States. Although he benefited from translators like Muna Lee, H. R. Hays, and Thomas Merton, other lesser translators were frequently anthologized. These poor translations tempered Carrera Andrade's brilliant metaphoric genius and were not representative of his work. After a number of years his poems were no longer being actively translated into English. Although he has become a forgotten poet among U.S. literary critics and anthologists, his reputation remains very high in France, Germany, Italy, and South America.

ORCHID IN THE HOT HOUSE
OF SOUTH AMERICAN LITERATURE

South American literature, like the garden in a hot house that produces new exotic species of flowers, has benefited from the artistic cross-pollination and experiments of the twentieth century. The poetic flowers that blossomed in the countries of the central and southern regions of the Americas are unmatched for their power, beauty and vibrancy. Such is the reputation of the South American poets that we know them today by name as we know Shakespeare: Borges, Huidobro, Neruda, Paz, Vallejo.

As part of the continuum of South American literature of the past century the poetry of Jorge Carrera Andrade exists like its own exotic orchid in the vibrant garden. His poetry is the perfect hybrid flower created from the marriage of European literary models and South American narrative, the experiments of modernism, lessons learned from the Imagists, the haiku he studied while posted in Japan, and the ever-present rural indigenous coloration of Ecuador. His best poems—minimalist portraits of rural life and his own encounters with the great cities of the world—benefit from their resonance with history. Jorge Carrera Andrade always composed his poems with the belief that he represented the New American, or, as he says in another poem, "the new angel of this [his] century."

STEVEN FORD BROWN
Paris, August 2000

CENTURY OF THE DEATH OF THE ROSE

I. Biografía

I. Biography

Biografía Para Uso de los Pájaros

Nací en el siglo de la defunción de la rosa
cuando el motor ya había ahuyentado a los ángeles.
Quito veía andar la última diligencia
y a su paso corrían en buen orden los árboles,
las cercas y las casas de las nuevas parroquias
en el umbral del campo
donde las lentas vacas rumiaban el silencio
y el viento espoleaba sus ligeros caballos.

Mi madre revestida de poniente
guardó su juventud en una honda guitarra
y sólo algunas tardes la mostraba a sus hijos
envuelta entre la música, la luz y las palabras.
Yo amaba la hidrografía de la lluvia,
las amarillas pulgas del manzano
y los sapos que hacían sonar dos o tres veces
su gordo cascabel de palo.

Sin cesar maniobraba la gran vela del aire.
Era la cordillera un litoral del cielo.
La tempestad venía, y al batir del tambor
cargaban sus mojados regimientos;
mas luego el sol con sus patrullas de oro
restauraba la paz agraria y transparente.
Yo veía a los hombres abrazar la cebada,
sumergirse en el cielo unos jinetes
y bajar a la costa olorosa de mangos
los vagones cargados de mugidores bueyes.

BIOGRAPHY FOR THE USE OF BIRDS

I was born in the century of the death of the rose
when the motor had already frightened away the angels.
Quito watched as the last stagecoach rolled away,
and at its passing trees ran by in perfect order,
fences and houses of new parishes,
at the threshold of the countryside
where slow cows were chewing silence
as wind spurred on its swift horses.

My mother, clothed in the setting sun,
stored her youth deep in a guitar,
and only on certain evenings would she show it to her children,
wrapped between music, light, and words.
I loved the hydrography of rain,
yellow fleas on apple trees,
and toads that made their thick wooden bells
ring two or three times.

The great sail of the air maneuvered ceaselessly.
The cordillera was a shore of the sky.
The storm came, and as drums rolled
its drenched regiments charged;
but then the sun's golden patrols
restored translucent peace to the land.
I watched men embrace barley,
horsemen sink into the sky,
and lowing oxen pull laden wagons down
to the mango-scented coast.

El valle estaba allá con sus haciendas
donde prendía el alba su reguero de gallos
y al oeste la tierra donde ondeaba la caña
de azúcar su pacífico banderín, y el cacao
guardaba en un estuche su fortuna secreta,
y ceñian, la piña su coraza de olor,
la banana desnuda su túnica de seda.

Todo ha pasado ya en sucesivo oleaje
como las vanas cifras de la espuma.
Los años van sin prisa enredando sus líquenes
y el recuerdo es apenas un nenúfar
que asoma entre dos aguas
su rostro de ahogado.
La guitarra es tan sólo ataúd de canciones
y se lamenta herido en la cabeza el gallo.
Han emigrado todos los ángeles terrestres,
hasta el ángel moreno del cacao.

There was the valley with its farms
where dawn set off a trail of roosters,
and to the west was the land where sugar cane
waved its peaceful banner, and cacao trees
stored in coffers their secret fortunes,
and the pineapple girded on its fragrant cuirass,
the nude banana its silken tunic.

It has all passed, in successive waves,
like useless ciphers of sea foam.
Entangled in lichens, the years go by slowly
and memory becomes scarcely a water-lily,
its drowned face
looming up between two waters.
The guitar is only a coffin for songs
as the rooster with its head wound laments.
All the earth's angels have emigrated,
even the dark brown angel of the cacao tree.

1937

Abril

Tiempo en que el corazón quiere saltar descalzo
y en que al árbol le salen senos como a una niña.
Nos asalta el deseo de escribir nuestras cosas
con pluma de golondrina.

Los charcos en el campo son copas de agua clara
que arruga un aletazo o un canuto de hierba
y es el aire de vidrio una marea azul
donde el lento barquito del insecto navega.

Chapotean a gusto las sandalias del agua.
Los mosquitos parece que ciernen el silencio
y los gorriones cogen en el pico la perla
del buen tiempo.

April

A time when the heart wants to skip barefoot
and trees grow breasts like a young girl.
A time when we are seized by the desire
to write things down with a swallow's feather.

These pools are no more than sips of clear water
rippled by a wing stroke or grass stem
and the glass air is a blue tide
the slow craft of an insect navigates.

Water sandals splash happily.
Mosquitoes appear to sieve the silence
and sparrows collect in their beaks
the pearl of good weather.

1928

Primavera y Compañia

El almendro se compra un vestido
para hacer la primera comunión. Los gorriones
anuncian en las puertas su verde mercancía.
La primavera ya ha vendido
todas sus ropas blancas, sus caretas de enero,
y sólo se ocupa de llevar hoy día
soplos de propaganda por todos los rincones.

Juncos de vidrio. Frascos de perfume volcados.
Alfombras para que anden los niños de la escuela.
Canastillos. Bastones
de los cerezos. Guantes muy holgados
del pato del estanque. Garza: sombrilla que vuela.

Máquina de escribir de la brisa en las hojas,
oloroso inventario.
Acudid al escaparate de la noche:
Cruz de diamantes, linternitas rojas
y de piedras preciosas un rosario.

Marzo ha prendido luces en la hierba
y el viejo abeto inútil se ha puesto anteojos verdes.
Hará la primavera, después de algunos meses,
un pedido de tarros de frutas en conserva,
uvas —glándulas de cristal dulce—
y hojas doradas para empacar la tristeza.

Spring & Co.

The almond tree has bought a dress
for first communion. Sparrows
in doorways advertise their green merchandise.
Spring has already sold
all of its white clothing, its January masks,
and today obsesses only with blowing
its propaganda into every corner.

Reeds of glass. Flasks of spilt perfume.
A carpet laid down for school children to walk on.
Little baskets. Batons
of cherry trees. Oversize gloves on
the duck in the pond. The stork: a flying parasol.

A typewriter breeze in the leaves,
a fragrant inventory.
Come to the display case of night:
cross of diamonds, little red lanterns,
and rosary of precious stones.

March has lit sparks in the grass;
the useless old spruce tree has put on green spectacles.
After these past few months Spring will prepare
an order of fruit jars of preserved
grapes—glands of sweet crystal—
and gilded leaves to store away sadness.

1928

Biografía

La ventana nació de un deseo de cielo
y en la muralla negra se posó como un ángel.
Es amiga del hombre
y portera del aire.

Conversa con los charcos de la tierra,
con los espejos niños de las habitaciones
y con los tejados en huelga.

Desde su altura, las ventanas
orientan a las multitudes
con sus arengas diáfanas.

La ventana maestra
difunde sus luces en la noche.
Extrae la raíz cuadrada de un meteoro,
suma columnas de constelaciones.

La ventana es la borda del barco de la tierra,
la ciñe mansamente un oleaje de nubes.
El capitán Espíritu busca la isla de Dios
y los ojos se lavan en tormentas azules.

La ventana reparte entre todos los hombres
una cuarta de luz y un cubo de aire.
Ella es, arada de nubes,
la pequeña propiedad del cielo.

Biography

The window was born of a desire for heaven.
And on the black wall it positioned itself like an angel:
it's friend to man,
a gatekeeper to the air.

It converses with puddles of the earth,
with childish mirrors of houses,
and tiled roofs on strike.

From high up, the windows
face the multitudes
with their diaphanous diatribes.

The main window
diffuses its light into the night.
It extracts the square root of a meteor,
totals columns of constellations.

The window is the gunwale of earth's ship;
a surf of clouds peacefully surrounds it.
The Captain Spirit looks for the island of God
and the eyes are washed clean in blue tempests.

The window divides among all men
a quart of light, a bucket of air.
The window, plowed by clouds,
is the small property of the sky.

1930

Jorge Carrera Andrade

Domingo

Iglesia frutera
sentada en una esquina de la vida.
Naranjas de cristal de las ventanas.
Órgano de cañas de azúcar.

Ángeles: polluelos
de la Madre María.

La campanilla de ojos azules
sale con los pies descalzos
a corretear por el campo.

Reloj de Sol.
Burro angelical con su sexo inocente.
Viento buenmozo del domingo
que trae noticias del cerro.
Indias con su carga de legumbres
abrazada a la frente.

El cielo pone los ojos en blanco
cuando sale corriendo de la iglesia
la campanilla de los pies descalzos.

SUNDAY

Fruit seller church
seated at the corner of life:
orange crystal windows,
the sugar cane organ.

Angels: little chicks
of Mother Mary.

The blue-eyed bell
wanders off bare foot
throughout the countryside.

Sun clock:
angelic burro with its innocent sex;
wind, in Sunday best,
brings news from the mountains.
Indian women with loads of vegetables
embracing foreheads.

The sky rolls its eyes
when it sees the church bell
run barefoot from the church.

                                        1929

La Extrema Izquierda

La compañera cigarra canta
con una astilla en la garganta.

Conspira entre la verdura
contra la humana dictadura.

Carrito dañado, tumbo a tumbo,
la cigarra marcha sin rumbo.

Predica y anda.
Es Secretaria de Propaganda.

Publica en una hoja de col:
La vida es dura y tuesta el sol.

Tienes razón, cigarra obrera
de minar el Estado con tu canto profundo.
Ambos formamos, compañera,
la extrema izquierda de este mundo.

THE EXTREME LEFT

Comrade cicada sings
with a splinter in its throat.

It conspires among all this greenness
against the human dictator.

A damaged little cart, tumbling and tumbling,
the cicada marches without direction.

Preaching and marching
it's the Secretary of Propaganda.

Its oratory is published on a cabbage leaf:
life is hard and burnt by the sun.

You have the right, working-class cicada,
to mine the State with your profound song.
We both form, Comrade,
the extreme left of the world.

1930

Discurso Anónimo

Camaradas: el mundo está construido sobre nuestros muertos
y nuestros pies han creado todas las rutas.
Mas, bajo el cielo de todos, no hay un palmo de sombra
para nosotros que hemos hecho florecer las cúpulas.

El pan, nieto rubio del sembrador, el techo
—fronda de barro y sol que cubre la familia—,
el derecho de amar y de andar no son nuestros:
Somos los negreros de nuestra propia vida.

La dicha, el mar que no hemos visito nunca,
las ciudades que jamás visitaremos
se alzan en nuestros puños cerrados como frutos
anunciando la más grave cosecha de los tiempos.

¡Sólo el derecho a morir, camaradas del mundo!
Cien manos se reparten las ofrendas del Globo.
Tiempo es ya de lanzarse a las calles y plazas
a rescatar la Obra construida por nosotros.

CENTURY OF THE DEATH OF THE ROSE

Anonymous Speech

Comrades: the world is built upon our dead
and our feet have created all the roads.
And beneath every sky, there is not an inch of shadow
for those of us who made the cupolas bloom.

Bread, blonde grandchild of the sower, a roof
—foliage of clay and sun that shelters the family—,
the right to love and walk freely are not ours:
we are the slave traders of our own lives.

Happiness, that sea we've never seen,
the cities we'll never visit,
we lift up in our clenched fists like fruit,
announcing the most serious harvest of all time.

Only the right to die, comrades of the world!
A hundred hands divide the offerings of the earth.
Already the time has come to hurl ourselves into
        the streets and plazas
to reclaim the Work we ourselves built.

1935

Mal Humor

Chimeneas de sombreros alados,
torcidas chimeneas, paréntesis del campo
en la ciudad, gargantas
por donde sube al cielo la canción de las cosas:
la canción familiar de la marmita,
del grillo y el fogón en la oscura cocina,
la canción de la silla de ruedas
y hasta el rumor monjil que hacen las puertas.

¡Chimeneas hostiles como armas
del odio de la urbe contra el azul que canta!
Humo sobre los techos: silenciosos disparos
contra el vuelo celeste de los pájaros.

Ascended a las nubes, apuntad los gorriones,
dejad la tierra oscura de los hombres.
Mi alma también es una chimenea
donde arde la canción de las vidas pequeñas,
chimenea de hollín
que exhala cada día sus palabras de humo
sobre el blanco papel del libro inédito.

Bad Humor

Chimneys with broad-brimmed hats,
twisted chimneys, parenthesis of country
in the city, throats
from which rises to the sky the song of things:
—the familiar song of the kettle,
the cricket, of the stove in a dark kitchen,
song of the rocking chair,
and even the nunlike murmur of opening doors.

Hostile chimneys like angry weapons
used by the city against the singing blue!
Smoke over roofs: a silent discharge
against the celestial flight of birds.

Rise to the sky, aim at sparrows,
abandon the dark land of men.
My soul, too, is a chimney
in which the song of small lives burns,
a sooty chimney
that exhales day after day its smoldering words
upon the white page of an unpublished book.

1926

El Huésped

En la gran puerta negra de la noche
dan doce aldabonazos.

Los hombres se incorporan:
con su escama de hielo les roza el sobresalto.

¿Quién será? Por las casas
 anda el miedo descalzo.

Los hombres ven su lámpara
apagarse al clamor de los aldabonazos:

llama el huésped desconocido
y una llamita azul les corre entre los párpados.

The Guest

Twelve knocks resound
against the huge black door of night.

Men sit up:
terror's icy scales glide over them.

Who will it be? Fear walks through
houses on bare feet.

Men see their lamps
extinguished by the noise of knocks:

an unknown guest calls;
a blue flicker runs along their eyelids.

1927

Poder de la Palabra

Tú, pantera y estatua, ángel de fruta,
sexual panadería, monumento de trigo,
con la garganta herida por el dardo
de una palabra súbita, en la sombra has caído.

¡Oh, palabra mortal que llega ardiendo
y se clava certera sobre el mármol
como el arma de fuego que, a distancia,
golpea ciegamente el cuerpo del soldado!

Tú, pantera de trigo, ahora yaces
estatua derribada en una playa sola.
Te rodea la espuma del olvido
¡oh tendida columna que habitan las palomas!

El relámpago azul de una palabra
ha dispersado inútiles tus alas y tus frutas
y, en la sombra, es tu cuerpo abandonado
fría panadería bañada por la luna.

Power of the Word

You, panther and statue, angel of fruit,
sexual bakery, monument of wheat,
with throat pierced by the dart
of a sudden word, have fallen into the shadows.

Oh, deadly word that arrives on fire
to engrave itself so accurately in marble,
like the weapon of fire that blindly strikes down
the soldier from a distance.

Panther of wheat, you now lie like
a toppled statue on an empty beach.
The sea foam of oblivion washes up around you—
Oh, prone pillars where doves nest!

Blue lightning of the word
has scattered your useless wings and fruit,
and, in shadows, your abandoned body is
a frigid bakery washed out by the moon.

1947

Edición de la Tarde

La tarde lanza su primera edición de golondrinas
anunciando la nueva política del tiempo,
la escasez de las espigas de la luz,
los navíos que salen a flote en el astillero del cielo,
el almacén de sombras del poniente,
los motines y desórdenes del viento,
el cambio de domicilio de los pájaros,
la hora de apertura de los luceros.

La súbita defunción de las cosas
en la marea de la noche ahogadas,
los débiles gritos de auxilio de los astros
desde su prisión de infinito y de distancia,
la marcha incesante de los ejércitos del sueño
contra la insurrección de los fantasmas
y, al filo de las bayonetas de la luz, el orden nuevo
implantado en el mundo por el alba.

EVENING EDITION

Evening casts forth its first edition of swallows
announcing new politics of the weather,
the scarcity of light's wheat,
ships that emerge to float in the sky's shipyard,
a warehouse of shadows from the west,
mutinies and disorders of the wind,
birds changing addresses,
the hour of the opening of brilliant stars.

The sudden death of things
drowning in the tide of night,
weak cries for help from stars
trapped in their prison of infinity and distance,
the incessant march of sleep armies
against an insurrection of ghosts,
and, at the edge of light's bayonets,
the new order imposed on the world by dawn.

                                        1935

Boletín del Mal Tiempo

El cielo del norte
levanta una bandera negra
en la barricada del horizonte.

No más oro del sol sobre los bancos.
¡Abajo el monopolio primaveral de flores!
Los carteles se amotinan
y la lluvia de finas bayonetas
alínea sus primeros escuadrones.

Ventarrón instaura un orden nuevo
en los paseos
y hace correr a los burgueses
hacia el refugio del aperitivo
en las esquinas reaccionarias.

Las casas se ponen
la escarapela roja del brasero
y en la ambulancia de las hojas muertas
capitula el buen tiempo.

BAD WEATHER BULLETIN

The northern sky
raises a black banner
on the barricade of the horizon.

No more golden sun on park benches.
Down with spring's monopoly of flowers!
Handbills mutiny
as thin bayonets of rain
line up their first squadrons.

Storm winds initiate a new order
on the boulevards,
forcing the bourgeoisie to run
for the refuge of apéritifs
in reactionary corners.

Houses turn on
red cockades of coals
and good weather capitulates
in the ambulance of dead leaves.

1928

Historia Contemporánea

Desde las seis está despierto el humo
que no cesa de señalar con su brazo la dirección del viento.
Los bancos conservan el sueño congelado de los vagabundos
y las vidrieras de los restaurantes aprisionan la calle
y la venden entre sus frutas, botellas y mariscos.
Un pájaro nuevo silba en las poleas
y en los andamios que cuelgan su columpio de los hombros
        de los edificios.
Los chicos suman panes y luceros en sus pizarras de luto
y los automóviles corren sin saber
que una piedra espera en una curva la señal del destino.

Ametralladora de palabras,
la máquina de escribir dispara contra el centinela invisible
        de la campanilla.
Los yunques fragmentan un sueño sonoro de herraduras
y las máquinas de coser aceleran su taquicardia de solteronas
entre el oleaje giratorio de las telas.

La tarde conduce un fardo de sol en un tranvía.

Obreros desocupados ven el cielo como una cesta de manzanas.
Regimientos de frío dispersan los grupos de vagabundos y mendigos.
El vendedor de pescado, los voceadores de periódicos
y el hombre que muele el cielo en su organillo
se dan la mano a la hora de la cena
en las cloacas y bajo el axila de los puentes
donde juegan al jardín los desperdicios

Contemporary History

Smoke awakens at six o'clock
to continuously signal with its arm the direction of the wind.
Benches retain the frozen sleep of vagrants
and restaurant windows capture the street
and sell it among fruits, bottles and shell-fish.
A new bird whistles in the pulleys and scaffolding
that hang from the shoulders of the building.
Children add loaves of bread and stars on their black slates
in mourning and cars drive by without knowing
that ahead a stone awaits in a curve for a sign of its destiny.

Machine-gun of words,
the typewriter
fires on the invisible sentinel of the bell.
Anvils break up the sonorous dream of horse shoes,
and amid turning waves of cloth
sewing machines accelerate the old maid's tachycardia.

Evening drives away a bundle of sunlight in a tram.

Unemployed laborers visualize the sky as a basket of apples.
Regiments of cold
disperse groups of vagrants and beggars.
The fish-vendor, the newspaper barkers,
and the man who grinds the sky in his organ
hold hands at dinner time
in the latrines and below the armpits of bridges
where garbage pretends to be a garden,

y sacan la lengua las latas de conserva.
Sus sombras crecen más allá de los tejados puntiagudos
y van cubriendo la ciudad, los caminos y los campos
próximos hasta ahogar en su pecho el relieve del mundo.

and empty cans stick out their tongues.
Shadows grow out beyond the pointed roofs,
gradually drowning the city, the roads, the nearby fields
until it smothers in its breast the world's relief.

1935

Soledad de las Cuidades

Sin conocer mi número.
Cercado de murallas y de límites.
Con una luna de forzado
y atada a mi tobillo una sombra perpetua.

Fronteras vivas se levantan
a un paso de mis pasos.

No hay norte ni sur, este ni oeste,
sólo existe la soledad multiplicada,
la soledad dividida para una cifra de hombres.
La carrera del tiempo en el circo del reloj,
el ombligo luminoso de los tranvías,
las campanas de hombros atléticos,
los muros que deletrean dos o tres palabras de color,
están hechos de una materia solitaria.

Imagen de la soledad:
el albañil que canta en un andamio,
fija balsa del cielo.
Imágenes de la soledad:
el viajero que se sumerge en un periódico,
el camarero que esconde un retrato en el pecho.

La ciudad tiene apariencia mineral.
La geometría urbana es menos bella
que la que aprendimos en la escuela.
Un triángulo, un huevo, un cubo de azúcar
nos iniciaron en la fiesta de las formas.

Loneliness of Cities

Without knowing my number,
enclosed by walls and borders,
I walk around with a prisoner's moon
and perpetual shadow chained to my ankle.

Living frontiers arise
a step beyond my footsteps.

There is neither north nor south, east nor west,
only a multiplied loneliness exists,
a loneliness divided by a cipher of men.
Time's race around the circus of the clock,
the luminous navel of streetcars,
bells with their athletic shoulders,
walls that spell out two or three colored words,
are made from the materials of loneliness.

Image of solitude:
bricklayer singing on a scaffold,
fixed raft in the sky.
Images of solitude:
a traveler submerged in a newspaper,
a waiter hiding a photograph in his vest pocket.

The city has a mineral appearance.
Urban geometry is less beautiful
than the geometry we learned at school.
A triangle, an egg, a cube of sugar
initiated us into a celebration of forms.

Sólo después fue la circunferencia:
la primera mujer y la primera luna.

¿Dónde estuviste, soledad,
que no te conocí hasta los veinte años?
En los trenes, los espejos y las fotografías
siempre estás a mi lado.

Los campesinos se hallan menos solos
porque forman una misma cosa con la tierra.
Los árboles son hijos suyos,
los cambios de tiempo observan en su propia carne
y les sirve de ejemplo la santoral de los animalitos.

La soledad está nutrida de libros,
de paseos, de pianos y pedazos de muchedumbre,
de ciudades y cielos conquistados por la máquina,
de pliegos de espuma
desenrollándose hasta el límite del mar.
Todo se ha inventado,
mas no hay nada que pueda librarnos de la soledad.

Los naipes guardan el secreto de los desvanes.
Los sollozos están hechos para ser fumados en pipa.
Se ha tratado de enterrar la soledad en una guitarra.
Se sabe que anda por los pisos desalquilados,
que comercia con los trajes de los suicidas
y que enreda los mensajes en los hilos telegráficos.

Circumferences only came later:
the first woman and the first moon.

Where were you, loneliness,
that I never knew you before I turned twenty?
On trains, in mirrors, in photographs,
you are always at my side now.

Country people are less lonely
because they are one with the land.
Trees are their sons,
they see weather changes in their own flesh,
and are taught by the saints' calendar of little animals.

The loneliness is nourished by books,
solitary walks, pianos, and fragments of crowds,
by cities and skies conquered by machines,
sheets of foam
unfolding toward the limits of the sea.
Everything has been invented,
but nothing has been invented to free us from loneliness.

Playing cards guard the secret of garrets.
Sobs are formed to be smoked away in a pipe.
There have been attempts to inter solitude in a guitar.
It's known that loneliness walks through vacant apartments,
has commerce with the clothing of suicides,
confuses messages in the telegraph wires.

1935

II. Lugar de Origen

II. Place of Origin

Lugar de Origen

Yo vengo de la tierra donde la chirimoya,
talega de brocado, con su envoltura impide
que gotee el dulzor de su nieve redonda,

y donde el aguacate de verde piel pulida
en su clausura oval, en secreto elabora
su substancia de flores, de venas y de climas.

Tierra que nutre pájaros aprendices de idiomas,
plantas que dan, cocidas, la muerte o el amor
o la magia del sueño o la fuerza dichosa,

animalitos tiernos de alimento y pereza,
insectillos de carne vegetal y de música
o de luz mineral o pétalos que vuelan,

capulí — la cereza del indio interandino —
codorniz, armadillo cazador, dura penca
al fuego condenada o a ser red o vestido,

eucalipto de ramas como sartas de peces
— soldado de salud con su armadura de hojas,
que despliega en el aire su batallar celeste —

son los mansos aliados del hombre de la tierra
de donde vengo, libre, con mi lección de vientos
y mi carga de pájaros de universales lenguas.

Place of Origin

I come from the land where the custard-apple,
a brocade bag, with its rind prevents
the spillage of its sweetness from the rounded snow,

and where the avocado with its polished green skin
in an oval cloister, secretly elaborates
its substance of flowers, veins and climates.

The land nurtures birds, apprentices of languages,
plants that cooked give death or love,
or the magic of dreams of joyous strength,

tender little animals of sustenance and laziness,
tiny insects of vegetal flesh and music,
mineral light, or petals that fly.

Capuli—cherry of the mid-Andean Indians—,
quail, hunter armadillo, hard plant leaves
condemned to burn or to be a net or garment,

eucalyptus branches like strings of fish
—robust soldier with an armor of leaves
deploying in the air his celestial struggle—,

these are the domesticated allies of mankind,
from where I come, free, with lessons from the winds
and my cargo of birds fluent in every language.

1947

Poema Hidrográfico

Los ríos se buscan por el mundo
y alargan en la tierra sus trompetas de vidrio.
Los mapas navegantes coleccionan
las biografías azules de los ríos.

Hidrografía ecuatorial
ilustrada de frutas de la tierra.
Ecuador: en tu aro de color
su pereza de loro dormita Suramérica.

Árboles litorales
cogidos por el lazo de la culebra boba.
Cocotero mulato de cintura flexible.
Bananero de intestinos rosas.

Bosques agujereados por los loros.
Vivienda de caña
del montuvio domador de mosquitos
y degollador de cocos de agua.

Bravos ríos serranos:
Aguas mordientes como espuelas
que hacen encabritar a los caballos.

Garabato infantil del puente
por donde pasa todas las mañanas
una india con un cántaro de leche.

Orillas orientales con pueblos de perdices,
tortugas de ojos de piedra,

Hydrographic Poem

Rivers seek each other throughout the world,
and spread throughout the earth their glass trumpets.
Navigation charts contain
the blue biographies of rivers.

Equatorial hydrography
illustrated with fruits of the earth.
Ecuador: in your ring of color,
South America sleeps in its parrot laziness.

Coastal trees
decorated with the bow of a silly snake.
Mulatto coconut trees with flexible waists.
Banana trees with rosy entrails.

Forests pierced by parrots.
Cane huts, homes of shore dwellers;
tamer of mosquitoes
and decapitator of coconuts.

Fierce mountain rivers:
waters that bite like spurs provoke
horses to rear up on hind feet.

Infant scribble on the bridge where
every morning an Indian woman passes
carrying a pitcher of milk.

Eastern shores populated by partridges.
Turtles with eyes of stone,

lavaderos de oro
y raíces paralíticas de ciencia.

Árbol de goma
— escalera de los nativos —
parada bajo el cielo con una herida honda.

Botes de madera salvaje
donde llevan fusiles y semillas
los rubios inmigrantes.

Corre un rumor de arados
junto a los grandes ríos.
Los colonos descalzos ven doblarse un arco iris
en la tierra peinada de surcos benditos.

Sierra de los ríos labradores,
Litoral de los ríos artesanos,
Oriente de los ríos misioneros:
¡sobre las aguas dulces echemos nuestros barcos!

gold washings,
and paralytic roots of science.

Rubber tree, with its deep wounds,
—staircase for Indians—,
stops just below the sky.

Boats of rough wood
in which blonde immigrants
carry rifles and seeds.

The booming sound of plows runs
along the big rivers.
Barefoot colonists see a rainbow reflected
in an earth combed with blessed furrows.

Mountain range of toiling rivers,
sea coast of artisan rivers,
Orient of missionary rivers,
let us launch our boats over the fresh waters!

1928

Cartel Electoral
del Verde

Verde marino, almirante de los verdes.
Verde terrestre, camarada de los labradores,
innumerable anticipo de la felicidad de todos,
cielo infinito del ganado que pasta frescas eternidades.

Luz submarina del bosquecillo
donde plantas, insectos y pájaros viven consumiéndose
en el amor callado de un dios verde.
Olor verde de la carnosa cabuya
que en su marmita vegetal elabora
un profundo licor
hecho de lluvia y sombra.

Mesa tropical donde suda con su penacho verde
la cabeza tatuada de la piña.
Arbustos de jorobas verdes,
parientes pobres de las colinas.

Verde música de los insectos que cosen sin cesar
el paño grueso de la grama,
los zancudos que habitan en los violines
y el redoblar del opaco tamborcillo verde de la rana.

La verde cólera del cacto
y la paciencia de los árboles que recogen en su red verde
una pesca milagrosa de pájaros.

Election Handbill
for Green

Marine green, admiral of greens,
terrestrial green, comrade of farmers,
numberless advance payments on everyone's happiness,
infinite sky of livestock grazing on cool eternities.

Thicket of submarine light
where plants, insects and birds live consuming themselves
in the silent love of a green god.
Green odor of fleshy agave
brewing in its vegetable cauldron,
a profound liquor
blended from rain and shadow.

Tropical plateau where the tattooed head
of a pineapple —with green plume— sweats.
Hunchbacked green shrubs,
poor relatives of the hills.

The green music of insects eternally sewing
a coarse cloth of conch grass,
where waders live in violins
amid the drumming of opaque little, green bullfrog drums.

A green anger of cactus,
the patience of trees that harvest in emerald nets
a miraculous catch of birds.

Todo el verde aplacador del mundo
ahogándose en el mar; trepando las montañas hasta el cielo
y corriendo en el río escuela de desnudez
y en la vaca nostálgica del viento.

All this green appeasement of the world,
drowning itself in the sea, climbing mountains to the sky,
running through the river —school for nudity—
and in the nostalgic cow which is the wind.

1935

Movimientos de la Naturaleza

Las cortezas escuchan el rasguñar de las plantas y de los insectos.
El viento rumia dulcemente entre los pastos.
Toma nota el estanque en su memoría
del parentesco que existe entre las más pequeñas nubes y los gansos.

En sus bodegas de sombra guardan en desorden los árboles
las boinas escolares de los hongos.
La noche escamotea el paisaje.
Un sideral labriego desparrama sus espigas de fósforo.

Movements of Nature

Tree-bark listens to the rustle of plants and insects
as wind softly ruminates through the field.
The pond takes down a note in its memory
of kinship between the smallest clouds and geese.

In their wineries of shadow, trees untidily store
schoolboy berets of mushrooms.
Night plays sleight-of-hand with the landscape.
A sidereal farmer scatters sheaves of light.

1947

SIERRA

Ahorcadas en la viga del techo
con sus alas de canario las mazorcas.

Conejillos de Indias
engañan al silencio analfabeto
con chillidos de pájaro y arrullos de paloma.

Hay en la choza una muda carrera
cuando el viento empuja la puerta.

La montaña brava
ha abierto su oscuro paraguas de nubes
con varillas de rayos.

Al Francisco, al Martín y al Juan
trabajando en la hacienda del cerro
les habrá sorprendido el temporal.

Un aguacero de pájaros
cae chillando en los sembrados.

SIERRA

Ears of corn, with canary wings,
hung from roof beams.

Guinea pigs
deceive the illiterate silence
with bird squeaks and a dove-like cooing.

There is a silent rustling in the hut
as wind pushes at the door.

The fierce mountain
has opened—with ribs of lightning—
its dark umbrella of clouds.

A downpour surprises
Francisco, Martin and Juan
working the mountain plantation.

A shower of birds
falls shrieking into the tilled fields.

1929

Canción Breve del Espantajo

El espantajo
un tráfico de brisas
ordena en los sembrados.

Cuida en el buen sol
la uva picada,
barril del gorrión.

En el circo del campo
danza y gesticula,
vegetal payaso.

Un ladrido azul
le da el horizonte:
mordiscos de luz.

Le invitan caminos
y le burlan pájaros
a vuelos y a silbos.

Y le da el ocaso
una cruz de sombra
al espantajo.

BRIEF SONG OF THE SCARECROW

The scarecrow,
in a traffic of breezes,
invokes order in the tilled fields.

In dazzling sunlight
he tends the bird-pecked grape,
wine cask for sparrows.

Vegetable clown:
in the circus of the fields
he dances and waves his arms.

The horizon
barks at him with blue:
bites of light.

Roads invite him.
With flutterings and whistles,
birds mock him.

Sunset bestows
a cross of shadow
upon the scarecrow.

1928

Corte de Cebada

En un cuerno vacío de toro
sopló el Juan el mensaje de la cebada lista.

En sus casas de barro
las siete familias
echaron un zumo de sol
en las morenas vasijas.

La loma estaba sentada en el campo
con su poncho a cuadros.

El colorado, el verde, el amarillo
empezaron a subir por el camino.

Entre un motín de colores
se abatían sonando las cebadas de luz
diezmadas por las hoces.

La Tomasa pesaba la madurez del cielo
en la balanza de sus brazos tornasoles.

Le moldeaba sin prisa la cintura
el giro lento del campo.

Hombres y mujeres de las siete familias,
sentados en lo tierno del oro meridiano,
bebieron un zumo de sol
en las vasijas de barro.

Barley Harvest

With a bull's hollow horn Juan
announces the ripening of the barley.

In clay huts
seven families pour
into brown jars
juice pressed from the sun.

A hill squats in a field
wrapped in a plaid poncho.

Red, green, yellow
begin to climb the road.

Amid a riot of colors,
a cacophony, the glowing barley
is cut down, decimated by sickles.

Tomasa weighs the ripeness of sky
on the scale of her light reflecting arms.

Slowly the field
encircles her waist.

Men and women of the seven families
seated in the soft gold of noon
drink fermented sun
from clay jars.

1929

Fiesta de San Pedro

Alazán, Alazán:
Después de la cena ciruela
a carrera tendida hacia el pueblo
de sombreros de paja del páramo.

El montado lleva en el ala del poncho
un rollo de viento.

Carteles estremecidos de gritos
en los estancos del camino.

Redobla en las orejas el viento tambor.
Corren en fila india los árboles del cerro.

Echa su lazo de hielo un aullido
a la garganta del silencio.

Con su peineta de luminarias
la primera casa del pueblo.

Han venido los peones de Santa Prisca
con sus ponchos color de ciruela:
borrachos de fuegos artificiales
se arriman al hombro de las puertas.

La Rueda chillona! La Rueda de luces! La Rueda!
Muere acribillada de cohetes
la noche de ojos de aguardiente.

Festival of San Pedro

Sorrel horse, sorrel horse:
After a meal of plums,
a mad gallop toward the village
roofed with straw hats from the highlands.

The horseman carries a roll of wind
in the wing of his poncho.

Shouts in the street ruffle handbills
posted on the windows of tobacco shops.

A drum roll of wind echoes in our ears.
Trees run Indian file up the hill.

A howl throws its lasso of ice
around the throat of silence.

The first house of the village
has a coiffure of lights.

The peons of Santa Prisca have come
in their plum-colored ponchos:
drunk on fireworks
they lean in the shoulders of doorways.

The Shouting Wheel! The Wheel of Lights! The Wheel!
Night with its brandy-colored eyes
dies pierced by rockets.

1929

Indiada

La garúa del monte
hace chillar las últimas candelas
rotas en resplandores.

Los comuneros llevan la mañana
enredada en los dientes de sus hoces
hacia la tierra baja.

En el vaho de los ponchos serranos
colorados como manzanas
aletean las voces y los pájaros.

Hacia la tierra gorda de gavillas,
en el ala cóncava de los sombreros
baja el viento del páramo.

Los caminos arrieros conducen en la noche
en los carros del aire
gavillas de canciones.

La indiada lleva la mañana
en la protesta de sus palas.

Indian Rebellion

The mountain's rainy mist
makes the last broken candles
hiss into brilliance.

Village Indians carry the morning
on the blades of their sickles
into the lowlands.

In steam from mountain ponchos,
the color of apples,
flutter birds and voices.

Wind from the highlands
descends in concave brims of hats
toward the lowlands, fat with sheaves.

In carts of air
mule driver roads carry clusters of songs
through the night.

The Indian rebellion carries morning
in the protest of their shovels.

1929

Fantasma de las Granjas

Mi sombra penetrada por los pastos con rocío
por las constelaciones prisioneras en las granjas
por la respiración de los hombres dormidos
en sus tumbas provisionales,
avanza hasta el camino descubridor de horizontes.
La angustia cósmica de las ranas me atraviesa.
Las ranas metafísicas dialogan con los astros.
Cada rana
monedero del silencio
pierde una a una
sus monedas de cobre.

El río desnudo baja de la montaña
como un arcángel con su armadura de cristal.
Escucha: el caballo levanta su casco herrado
y lo hunde en el agua de los sueños
con lentitud semejante a la danza.

Tierra amada: te siento vivir dentro de mí
con la totalidad de tus formas y seres.
El rumor de tus árboles circula entre mis huesos.
Mientras todo duerme
laboro como una abeja en las colmenas del espíritu.

THE GHOST OF FARMHOUSES

My shadow, penetrated by dewy pastures,
by constellations imprisoned in farmhouses,
by the breathing of sleeping men
in their temporary tombs,
advances down a road that discovers horizons.
The cosmic anguish of frogs pierces me.
The metaphysical frogs converse with the stars.
Each frog, counterfeiter of silence,
loses, one by one,
its copper coins.

Beneath the mountain is a nude river
like an archangel in its crystal suit of armor.
Listen: the horse lifts its iron hoof
and with slow dance-like movements
plunges it into the water of dreams.

Beloved land: I feel you living inside me
with the totality of your shapes and beings.
The murmur of your trees circulates in my bones.
While everything around me sleeps,
I work like a bee in the hives of the spirit.

1966

El Gallo de la Catedral

El gallo de la veleta
no puede batir sus alas
aunque es hoy día de fiesta.

El sol extiende en el atrio
su gran alfombra amarilla
al paso de Ana del Campo.

Colchas de oro en los balcones
y diamantes en los techos
en las cúpulas y torres.

Ana del Campo ha venido
con su lozano semblante
de doncella del rocío.

Quisiera cantar el gallo
pobre don Juan de hojalata
subido en el campanario.

Las nubes le hacen la rueda
en su gallinero azul,
y el gallo ardiente llamea.

Gallo de plata en el viento,
gallo de sol, paralítico
en un desierto de techos.

Asceta catedralicio,
no sabe de otro maíz

Weather Vane on the Cathedral

Even though today is fiesta day
the rooster of the weathervane
can't flap its wings.

As Ana del Campo passes through
the sunlight spreads in the courtyard
its great yellow carpet.

Golden quilts on balconies,
diamonds on roofs,
cupolas and turrets.

Ana del Campo has come
with her lush countenance
like the maid of dew.

The rooster, poor tin Don Juan,
would like to sing
up in its church tower.

As clouds wheel around him
in his blue hen house,
the burning rooster flares.

Silver rooster in the wind,
sun cock, paralyzed
among a desert of roofs.

Cathedral ascetic,
who knows no other grain

que el celeste del granizo.

Y al paso de Ana del Campo
cambia señales de luz
con su amigo el pararrayo.

•

Ana: guíame a la puerta
de tu morada de flores
donde la dicha es eterna.

Dame tu fresco rocío
para mi arenal sediento.
Dame tu campo de lirios.

Ana del Campo, campana
de fiesta mayor, ayúdame
a subir todas las gradas

hasta las supremas luces.
¡Por tu amor yo te daré
toda mi hacienda de nubes!

than celestial hailstones.

As Ana del Campo passes
he exchanges signals of light
with his friend the lightning rod.

•

Ana: guide me to the door
of your house of flowers
where happiness is eternal.

Give me your cool dew
for my sandy thirst.
Give me your field of lilies.

Ana del Campo, bell
of the grand fiesta, help me
climb all these steps

to the supreme lights.
For your love I will give you
my entire hacienda of clouds!

1928

Juan Sin Cielo

Juan me llamo, Juan Todos, habitante
de la tierra, más bien su prisionero,
sombra vestida, polvo caminante,
el igual a los otros, Juan Cordero.

Sólo mi mano para cada cosa
—mover la rueda, hallar hondos metales—
mi servidora para asir la rosa
y hacer girar las llaves terrenales.

Mi propiedad labrada en pleno cielo
—un gran lote de nubes era mío—
me pagaba en azul, en paz, en vuelo
y ese cielo en añicos: el rocío.

Mi hacienda era el espacio sin linderos
—oh territorio azul siempre sembrado
de maizales cargados de luceros—
y el rebaño de nubes, mi ganado.

Labradores los pájaros: el día
mi granero de par en par abierto
con mieses y naranjas de alegría.
Maduraba el poniente como un huerto.

Mercaderes de espejos, cazadores
de ángeles llegaron con su espada
y, a cambio de mi hacienda—mar de flores—
me dieron abalorios, humo, nada . . .

Juan Without Sky

Juan they call me, Juan Everyman, citizen
of the earth, more like its prisoner,
clothed in shadows, a walking speck of dust
equal to all other men, I am Juan Doe.

Just my hand for each thing
—driving the wheel, discovering hidden metals—
my servant for picking the rose,
and also for turning the key in the world's door.

I worked my tilled land in a vast sky
— a large profit of clouds was mine —
paid to me in blue, in peace, in flight,
and that sky in pieces: the dew.

My farmland was an expanse without borders
—oh, blue territory, always sown
like cornfields laden with brilliant stars—
and this flock of clouds, my livestock.

Birds were my farmhands; the clear day
a wide open storehouse
full of grain and joyful oranges.
The sunset ripening like a garden.

Merchants of mirrors, hunters
of angels arrived with swords
and in exchange for my farmland —that sea of flowers—
they gave me glass beads, smoke, nothing. . .

Los verdugos de cisnes, monederos
falsos de las palabras, enlutados,
saquearon mis trojes de luceros,
escombros hoy de luna congelados.

Perdí mi granja azul, perdí la altura
—reses de nubes, luz recién sembrada—
¡toda una celestial agricultura
en el vacío espacio sepultada!

Del oro del poniente perdí el plano
—Juan es mi nombre, Juan Desposeído—
En lugar del rocío hallé el gusano
¡un tesoro de siglos he perdido!

Es sólo un peso azul lo que ha quedado
sobre mis hombros, cúpula de hielo. . .
Soy Juan y nada más, el desolado
herido universal, soy Juan sin Cielo.

Murderers of swans, counterfeiters
of words, men dressed in black,
looted my granary of radiant stars,
leaving today only a frozen wreckage of moon.

I lost my blue farmland, lost it in the heights
—my herd of clouds, the newly sown light—
all that celestial agriculture
buried in empty space!

I lost the map to the gold of the sunset
—Juan is my name, Juan the Dispossessed—
Instead of dew at dawn, I discovered the worm,
a treasure accumulated over centuries lost!

Only a blue weight on my shoulders is left—
an ice cupola on my shoulders . . .
I am Juan, and nothing more, the desolate one,
wounded universally, I am Juan without Sky.

1950

Invectiva Contra la Luna

Yo podría decir: Luna, fruto de hielo
en las ramas azules de la noche.
Pero tantos sollozos se esconden en las piedras,
tantos combates mudos se libran en la sombra,
que yo digo: la luna es sólo un pozo
de llanto de los hombres.

Tantas lágrimas ruedan por las tumbas,
tantas lágrimas corren por el hambre
de ojos ya sin edad, desde hace siglos,
que la lluvia no cesa sobre el mundo
y yo veo tan sólo la harina de la luna
y su plato vacío y su mortaja.

Yo podría decir: La luna es una mina
de plata fabulosa,
la luna de paseo va con sus guantes blancos
a coger margaritas. Pero hay tantos difuntos
sin flores, tantos niños con las manos heladas
que yo digo: La luna es el Polo del cielo.

Bruja azul, encantaba el sueño de los hombres,
inventaba el primer amor de las doncellas,
andaba por los bosques con chinelas de vidrio
en los tiempos felices. La luna era una almohada
de plumas arrancadas a los ángeles
para dormir la eternidad celeste.

Luna: arroja tu máscara en el agua,
reparte tus harinas, tus sábanas, tus panes

INVECTIVE AGAINST THE MOON

I could say: moon, icy fruit
in the blue branches of night.
But so many cries are hidden away in stones,
so many quiet battles are fought in the shadows
that I say: the moon is only a well
of human tears.

So many tears roll through graveyards,
so many tears flow from hunger,
from ageless eyes, for centuries,
that rains on this earth will never cease.
And all I see is the moon's white flour,
its empty plate and shroud.

I could say: the moon is a mine
of fabulous silver,
or the moon promenades in white gloves
on its way to gather daisies. But there are so many
dead without flowers, so many children have frozen hands,
that I say: the moon is North Pole of the sky.

Blue witch, bewitching dreams of men,
invented a young virgin's first love,
and, in joyful times, wandered through
a forest in glass slippers. The moon
was a feather pillow pluckered from the angels
to sleep on for celestial eternity.

Moon, throw your mask in the water,
distribute your white flour, your sheets,

JORGE CARRERA ANDRADE

entre todos los hombres.
No seas sólo un pozo de lágrimas, un témpano
o un islote de sal, sino un granero
para el hambre infinita de la tierra.

your bread among the people.
No longer be a pool of tears, an iceberg,
or an island of salt, but a granary
for the infinite hunger of the earth.

1957

III. Seres Elementales

III. Elemental Things

El Objeto y su Sombra

Arquitectura fiel del mundo,
Realidad, más cabal que el sueño.
La abstraccíon muere en un segundo:
sólo basta un fruncir del ceño.

Las cosas. O sea la vida.
Todo el universo es presencia.
 La sombra al objeto adherida
¿acaso transforma su esencia?

Limpiad el mundo—ésta es la clave—
de fantasmas del pensamiento.
Que el ojo apareje su nave
para un nuevo descubrimiento.

The Object and its Shadow

Faithful architecture of the world,
reality, more complete than dream.
Abstraction dies in a second:
only enough to wrinkle a frown.

Things. Or life itself.
The whole universe is presence.
Can a shadow that adheres to an object
transform its essence?

Cleanse the world — this is the key —
of the ghosts of thought.
Let the eye prepare its vessel
for a new discovery.

1929

Tres Estrofas al Polvo

Tu roce de ceniza va gastando las formas,
hermano de la noche y la marea.
Envuelves todo objeto en una muerte anónima
que es tan sólo un regreso a su origen de tierra.

Escalas sin ser visto muros y corredores.
Palidecen los trajes ahorcados
en sus perchas de sombra y los relojes
cesan súbitamente de vivir a tu paso.

Clandestino emisario de las ruinas,
modelas en las cosas tu máscara terrestre.
Nada puede escapar a tu parda conquista,
aliado innumerable de la muerte.

Three Stanzas to Dust

Brother of night and tides,
your ashen touch goes wearing forms.
You envelop each object in an anonymous death
which is only a return to earthly origins.

You walk unseen through corridors and walls.
As you pass by the hanged suits pale
in their closets of shadows
and clocks suddenly die.

Clandestine emissary of ruin,
molding everything to your terrestrial mask.
Incalculable ally of death,
nothing escapes your brown conquest.

1947

Vocación del Espejo

Cuando olvidan las cosas su forma y su color
y, acosados de noche, los muros se repliegan
y todo se arrodilla, o cede o se confunde,
sólo tú estás de pie, luminosa presencia.

Impones a las sombras tu clara voluntad.
En lo oscuro destella tu mineral silencio.
Como palomas súbitas
a las cosas envías tus mensajes secretos.

Casa silla se alarga en la noche y espera
un invitado irreal ante un plato de sombra,
y sólo tú, testigo transparente,
una lección de luz repites de memoría.

Vocation of the Mirror

When things forget form and color
and, pursued by night, walls retire
and everything kneels, yields, or is confused,
only you, luminous presence, remain awake.

You impose a transparent will on shadows.
Your mineral silence shimmers in darkness.
Like sudden doves
you send out secret messages to everything.

Chairs, grown taller in the dark, wait for
an unreal guest to be seated before a plate of shadow,
but only you, transparent witness,
can repeat from memory a lesson of light.

1937

El Reloj

Reloj:
picapedrero del tiempo.

Golpea en la muralla más dura de la noche,
pica tenaz, el péndulo.

La despierta vainilla
compone partituras de olor en los roperos.

Vigilando el trabajo del reloj
anda con sus pantuflas calladas el silencio.

The Clock

Clock:
stonecutter of time.

Obdurate chisel, pendulum,
strikes the hardest wall of night,

The awakened vanilla
composes a suite of fragrances in the armoire.

Observer of the clock's work,
silence moves about in hushed slippers.

1927

Espejo de Comedor

A Alfonso Reyes

Con escuadras y figuras
de cándida geometria,
el espejo de comedor edifica.

Iza planos palpitantes
hasta su nivel azul.
Toma medida de las cosas
con sus compases de luz.

Baraja certidumbres.
Esgrime diámetros.
Enfila luces.

Hiere su regla de cristal
la botella de agua, desnuda,
y un chorro oblicuo de diamantes
mana hasta la mesa oscura.

Los objetos
mueven en los hilos del aire
su telegrafía de reflejos.

Los colores estallan.
En las aristas felices
la luz bate sus pestañas.

Piscina vertical
con diagonales de hielo.

DINING ROOM MIRROR

To Alfonso Reyes

The dining room mirror
builds squares and
figures of incandescent geometry.

It hoists wavering planes
to its blue level.
It measures objects
with compasses of light.

It shuffles certainties.
Fences diameters.
Threads lights.

Its crystal ruler breaks
the nude water bottle
and a slanting stream of diamonds
flows toward the dark table.

Objects propel
their telegraphy of reflections
along cables of air.

Colors explode.
From euphoric bevels
light strikes its eyelashes.

Vertical pool
with diagonals of ice.

Gemelos con la vida
los senos virginales del frutero.

Mundo animado
de resplandeciente conciencia.
Trigonometría de luces.
Visuales ideas.

La vida cortada en normas:
el salero es sapiencia;
las ostras, memoria.

La pera es escultura
en los moldes del aire;
el café, inteligencia
y el azucarero un ángel.

Counterparts to life,
virginal breasts of the fruit bowl.

World animated by
a glittering consciousness,
a trigonometry of light,
visual ideas.

Life sliced into patterns:
the salt shaker, wisdom;
oysters, memory.

The pear is sculpted
into molds of air;
the coffee, intelligence,
and the sugar bowl, an angel.

1930

No Hay

En las librerías no hay libros,
en los libros no hay palabras,
en las palabras no hay esencia:
hay sólo cáscaras.

Lienzos pintados y fetiches
hay en los museos y salas.
En la Academia hay sólo discos
para las más fluriosas danzas.

En las bocas hay sólo humo,
en los ojos sólo distancias.
Hay un tambor en cada oído.
En la mente bosteza el Sahara.

Nada nos libra del desierto.
Del tambor nada nos salva.
Libros pintados se deshojan,
leves cáscaras de la Nada.

Nothing

In bookstores there are no books,
in books no words,
in words no essence:
there are only husks.

In museums and waiting rooms
there are painted canvases and fetishes.
In the Academy there are only recordings
for the wildest dances.

In mouths there is only smoke,
in the eyes only distance.
There is a drum in each ear.
A Sahara yawns in the mind.

Nothing frees us from the desert.
Nothing saves us from the drum.
Painted books shed their pages,
becoming husks of Nothing.

1966

La Cifra

En el orbe del cero
duerme el dios de los números,
pequeño dios que crea
de la nada los mundos.

¿Ilusión? En miríadas
la unidad multiplica.
Cero: ¿eres nada o todo?
De ti nace la cifra.

Números en millares:
infinita colmena.
Labran su miel mental
las abstractas abejas.

En arenas y en astros
su transparente círculo
esconde el cero eterno
¡oh, huevo del guarismo!

Mago de los espejos,
dios del número: ábreme
tu cueva de tesoros,
tu caja de caudales.

¡Cuánta riqueza oculta!
Aun los signos solos
multiplican las cosas:
El Número es de oro.

THE NUMBER

In the circle of the zero
sleeps the god of numbers,
a small god that creates
worlds from nothing.

An illusion? In myriads
unity multiplies.
Zero: are you nothing or everything?
You give birth to the number.

Numbers in thousands:
infinite hive.
Abstract bees cultivating
their mental honey.

In sand and stars
its transparent circle
conceals an eternal zero
Oh, egg of the numeral!

Magician of mirrors,
god of the number: open for me
your cave of treasures,
your box of riches.

How much hidden wealth!
Even the signs alone
can multiply things:
the Number is like gold.

JORGE CARRERA ANDRADE

Aves, peces, insectos,
árboles, piedras: números.
Sin el pequeño dios
no existiría el mundo.

Birds, fish, insects,
trees, stones: numbers.
Without this small god
nothing in the world could exist.

1958

SUMA

El molino de viento, el tambor y la rosa.
El acordeón, el cubo de agua y el espantajo.
La escalera de las gallinas y el sombrero sin sombra.
El muro donde el sol pega su cartel blanco.

La pala que voltea volúmenes idénticos
y los pájaros de color que maduran sobre las ramas.
El aire que vive su sueño en la cristalería
y el bastón que se enrosca en la silla de paja.

Las lechugas que van al río en orden escolar.
Las caperuzas subterráneas de los rábanos.
La regadera, el nido y los hongos de la madera:
Cifras verdes, sumandos animados.

Sum

Windmill, drum, and rose,
accordion, water-pail, scarecrow;
chickencoop ladder, sombrero without shade,
wall where sun hangs its white posters.

Shovel that turns over identical volumes,
and brilliant birds that ripen on branches.
Air that lives out its dreams in glassware,
and the walking stick hooked to a wicker-bottomed chair.

Lettuce marching down river like schoolchildren.
Radishes: Red Riding Hoods living underground.
Watering-pot, nest, fungi on wood:
green numbers, animated sums.

1935

Vida del Grillo

Inválido desde siempre,
ambula por el campo
con sus muletas verdes.

Desde las cinco
el chorro de la estrella
llena el pequeño cántaro del grillo.

Trabajador, con las antenas hace
cada día su pesca
en los ríos del aire.

Por la noche, misántropo,
cuelga en su casa de hierba
la lucesita de su canto.

¡Hoja enrollada y viva,
la música del mundo
conserva dentro escrita!

LIFE OF THE GRASSHOPPER

Always an invalid
he wanders through the field
on green crutches.

Since five o'clock
the stream from a star
has filled the grasshopper's tiny pitcher.

A laborer, he fishes
each day with his antenna
in rivers of air.

A misanthrope, at night
he hangs the flicker of his chirp
in a house of grass.

Leaf rolled up and alive,
the grasshopper keeps the music
of the world written inside!

1928

Canción de la Manzana

Cielo de tarde en miniatura
amarillo, verde, encarnado
 con luceros de azúcar
y nubecillas de raso,

manzana de seno duro
con nieves lentas para el tacto,
ríos dulces para el gusto,
cielos finos para el olfato.

Signo del conocimiento.
Portadora de un mensaje alto:
La ley de la gravitación
o la del sexo enamorado.

Un recuerdo del paraíso
es la manzana en nuestras manos.
Cielo minúsculo: en su torno
un ángel de olor está volando.

Song of the Apple

Afternoon sky in miniature:
yellow, green, flesh-colored
with bright stars of sugar,
tiny satin clouds.

Hard-breasted apple
with snows slow to the touch,
rivers sweet to the taste,
skies delicate to the smell.

Symbol of knowledge.
Bearer of a higher message:
the law of gravity
or the enamored sex.

The apple in our hands
is the memory of paradise.
Minuscule sky: in its curve
an angel of fragrance is flying.

1928

Dios de Alegría

Dios de alegría:
Te entreví
en pleno día.

La túnica de luz
se enredaba en el árbol
sin memoria de cruz.

Tu paso de cristal
bajaba la escalera
del manantial.

El cielo sonreía.
Iban flor y guijarro
en buena compañía.

Todo era lenguaje
divino.
Cada ala era un viaje

hacia el Dios de alegría
todo luz.
El mundo ardía.

God of Joy

God of joy,
I glimpsed you
in broad daylight.

A robe of light
enfolded the tree
without memory of the cross.

Your crystal footsteps
descended the well's
staircase.

The sky smiled;
flower and pebble
shared good company.

Everything was divine
language.
Each wing was a journey

toward all light,
God of joy.
The world was on fire.

1966

El Desayuno del Mundo

Las cuatro horas—desnudas niñas—
parten en cuatro tajadas
la mañana de sandía.

Un ojo azul se abre en la altura.
Aprenden los niños del mundo
 el Catecismo del azucar.

Del teatro de terciopelo de la noche
salen las ventanas
con los ojos bañados en lágrimas.

Los relojes no cesan de cantar
 su canto de polilla
en un huequito de la eternidad.

Van haciéndose agua
en el cielo de sandía
 las estrellas azucaradas.

Toma el mundo recién lavado
sus cucharadas de luz
con rebanadas de campo.

The World's Breakfast

The four hours—nude girls—
slice the watermelon of morning
into four portions.

A blue eye opens at the zenith.
The world's children learn
the Catechism of sugar.

Eyes bathed in tears,
windows emerge
from the velvet theater of night.

Clocks go on singing
their moth-like song
in a little hollow of eternity.

Sugar-sprinkled stars
turn to water
in a watermelon sky.

The newly washed world
takes spoonfuls of light
with slices of meadow.

1930

Octubre

Octubre: nuez, manzana de los meses.
Tu madurez fulgura
en las últimas mieses,
ruinas de una dorada arquitectura.

Tu carne aérea, tu ala desplegada
laten en plumas frías,
Ave inmensa, cazada
servida en un festín treinta y un días.

Los números terrestres son iguales
en tu niveladora y final cuenta:
hojarascas—caídos ventanales—,
nueces—leve osamenta—.

De tanta fruta vana, rodadora
y hoguera pisoteada
apenas queda ahora
tu íntima brasa, almendra concentrada.

Octubre de reserva y de justicia
y de sombrío paño
que sucede al color de la delicia,
oh poniente del año.

Después de nueve meses de camino
llegas, la pompa anual desvanecida,
mercader vespertino
con tu peso y medida.

October

October: nut and apple of the months,
ruins of a gilded architecture,
your ripeness gleams
in the last sheaves.

Your airy flesh, wing unfurled,
flutters in cold plumage,
a huge bird, hunted
and served in a thirty-one day feast.

In the final leveling and accounting
the earthly numbers are equal:
dead leaves, fallen shutters,
nuts, frail bones.

So much wasted fruit left over on the ground,
an extinguished bonfire,
almost nothing left but your ember
your concentrated almond.

October of justice and reticence,
and month at somber cloth
that follows the color of delight,
oh, sunset of the year!

The year's splendor vanquished,
after nine months of travel you arrive,
vespertine merchant,
with your weights and measures.

1939

Taller del Tiempo

Herrero del otoño: forja mi corazón,
da forma a su racimo en tu yunque de oro.
A cada golpe gime el metal del olvido.
Al soplo de la fragua arden hasta las nubes.

Soy un hombre vestido de hojas secas.
Mi pecho abriga líquenes de fuentes extinguidas.
El pájaro hablador de otro tiempo cantaba:
"El mundo es tuyo. Tómalo. La luz marca tu frente."

Yo te grité mi amor, Naturaleza impávida,
ciega de ojos azules, sorda de nube y rocas.
Nada me diste, sólo la deseada manzana:
un mes de paraíso, cien años de serpiente.

Nada más que el arco iris en su jaula de lluvia
y la rosa que expira en su cruz de perfume.
El mundo entero gime en el yunque otoñal
El fuego inexorable consume la hojarasca.

Bosque andrajoso, pierdes tus remiendos dorados
por obra del otoño, mal aprendiz de sastre.
Un reloj de corteza mide el tiempo del árbol.
El mirlo anuncia el juicio final de las hormigas.

Ablanda, forjador otoñaI, en el yunque
mi corazón forrado del metal del olvido.
Dale una oscura forma de escarcela de lágrimas.
A cada golpe tiembla un nido de palomas.

Time's Workshop

Autumnal blacksmith: forge my heart,
give shape to its cluster upon your golden anvil.
At each blow metals of forgetfulness moan.
Even clouds burn with each breath of the bellows.

I am a man dressed in dry leaves.
My breast harbors moss from extinguished fountains.
A talking bird from another time used to sing:
"The world is yours. Take it. Light brands your forehead."

I shout my love to you, impassive Nature,
blind of blue eyes, deaf of clouds and rocks.
You gave me nothing, only the desired apple:
a month of paradise, a hundred years of serpent.

Nothing more than a rainbow in its cage of rain,
and the rose that expires on its cross of perfume.
The whole world moans on the autumnal anvil
as an inexorable fire consumes the fallen leaves.

Tattered forest, you lose your golden rags
to the labor of autumn, that unskilled tailor's apprentice.
A tree's time measured by the bark's clock,
and the last judgment of ants announced by a blackbird.

Autumnal blacksmith, soften on the anvil
my heart forged from metals of forgetfulness.
As at each hammer blow a dove's nest trembles.
Give it the dark shape of a box filled with tears.

JORGE CARRERA ANDRADE

A cada golpe tiembla mi corazón atado
a su yunque en la última hoguera de la tarde.
Las brasas esparcidas arden en las ventanas.
Sobre mi frente el tiempo avienta las cenizas.

My heart, fastened to its anvil, in the last blaze
of twilight, trembles at each blow.
A scattering of embers glows in the windows.
Upon my forehead time fans the ashes.

1958

IV. Boletines de Viaje

IV. Traveler's Bulletins

Boletín de Viaje

Sobre el tejado del mundo
puso el gallo a secar su canto de colores.
La luz era pesada como un fruto.

Sus tablas de la ley me entregó el campo.
De la antigua madera de la cruz
estaba hecho el arado.

Era un anillo de dolor
la línea ecuatorial
en el dedo del corazón.

En la nave de veinte cornetas
embarqué mi baúl de papagayos
hacia otro extremo de la tierra.

Ardía el alfabeto de las constelaciones.
Giraban gozosos los puertos niños
en el carrusel del horizonte.

Se amotinaron los mares
 y los cuatro vientos
contra mi sueño almirante.

Ancla: Trébol de hierro.
Te arrojó el Capitán al continente antiguo.
Vi las torres cargadas con sus sacos de nubes
y las grúas cigüeñas
con su cesta en el pico.

Traveler's Bulletin

Over the tiled roof of the world
the rooster hung its brightly colored song out to dry.
The light was heavy like fruit.

The countryside handed me its tablets of law;
the plow was made from the same
ancient wood of the Cross.

The equatorial line was
a ring of grief
on the finger of the heart.

On a ship with twenty foghorns,
I launched my trunk of parrots
toward the other end of the world.

An alphabet of constellations burned.
Harbors, like children, whirled gaily
on the carousel of the horizon.

Seas and the four winds
mutinied
against my admiral dreams.

Anchor: iron cloverleaf.
The captain cast you off onto an ancient continent.
I saw towers laden with sacks of clouds
and cranes, storks
with baskets in their beaks.

Europa hacía andar con ritmo de aceite
los arados mecánicos.
Con su pajita tornasol
la espiga chupaba el calcio.

Mas toda la alegría del mundo
al subir por las chimeneas
se convertía en humo.

En la hoja blanca de la harina
imprimían los molinos
la arenga proletaria de la espiga.

Las ciudades se hablaban a lo largo del aire.
Descubrí al hombre. Entonces
comprendí mi mensaje.

Europe made the mechanical plows walk
with a rhythm of oil.
Through its iridescent straw
wheat absorbed calcium from the earth.

But all the world's happiness
rising through chimneys
was converted into smoke.

On blank pages of flour
mills were printing
the wheat's proletarian oratory.

Cities were conversing through the air.
I discovered man. Then
I understood my message.

                                        1930

El Hombre del Ecuador
Bajo la Torre Eiffel

Te vuelves vegetal a la orilla del tiempo.
Con tu copa de cielo redondo
y abierta por los túneles del tráfico,
eres la ceiba máxima del Globo.

Suben los ojos pintores
por tu escalera de tijera hasta el azul.
Alargas sobre una tropa de tejados
tu cuello de llama del Perú.

Arropada en los pliegues de los vientos,
con tu peineta de constelaciones,
te asomas al circo
de los horizontes.

Mastil de una aventura sobre el tiempo.

Orgullo de quinientos treinta codos.

Pértiga de la tienda que han alzado los hombres
en una esquina de la historia.
Con sus luces gaseosas
copia la vía láctea tu dibujo en la noche.

Primera letra de un Abecedario cósmico,
apuntada en la dirección del cielo,
esperanza parada en zancos,
glorificación del esqueleto.

Ecuadorian Man
Under the Eiffel Tower

You turn into a plant on the coast of time.
With a chalice of round sky
and opening for traffic tunnels,
you are the largest ceiba tree on earth.

The painter's eye climbs up
through your scissor-stairs to blue.
Over a flock of roofs you stretch your neck
like a llama of Peru.

Robed in folds of wind,
with an ornamental comb of constellations,
you loom over
the circus of the horizon.

Mast of an adventure upon time!

Pride of five hundred and thirty feet.

Pole of the tent raised by men
in a corner of history.
With gaseous lights the Milky Way
reproduces your stretch of night.

First letter of a cosmic Alphabet,
pointing towards the sky,
hope standing on stilts,
a glorified skeleton.

Hierro para marcar el rebaño de nubes
o mudo centinela de la edad industrial.
La marea del cielo
mina en silencio tu pilar.

Iron that brands a flock of clouds,
mute sentinel of the Industrial Age.
The tides of heaven
silently undermine your column.

1930

Les Halles

Mercado Central de Paris

Camiones repletos de violetas
mojados de lluvia y cantos de gallos
entran por las puertas de París todas las madrugadas
sembrando lunas y relámpagos en los charcos
y salen por las mismas puertas en pleno día
colmados de sombra
después de abandonar sobre las aceras
su cargamento de campo amasado con sol.
Llevadme, camiones enmohecidos
al paraíso de la cebolla y las trenzas rubias
donde yo pueda lavar mis ojos
para ver un mundo enjoyado de rocío.

Pesad, pesad el pescado y las lechugas
pesad la luna entera
pesad los corazones azucarados por libras
las lágrimas por litros,
pesad una ensalada de sueños
sacad de los camiones todo el amor del mundo
toda la carga pura
preparada por meses de trabajo
y por la paciencia fecundante del agua.

La cigüeña del aceite picotea la luna
cuando las sombras devoran los últimos caballos blancos.
Digo cigüeña mi mente responde estaño
mientras un río relumbra en la ventana
sin poder entrar.

Les Halles

Central Market, París

Trucks packed with violets,
soaked by rain and songs of crowing roosters,
enter the gates of Paris each dawn,
sowing moons and lightning in puddles,
and leave through the same gates at noon
overflowing now with shadows,
after abandoning upon sidewalks
a cargo of country kneaded with sunlight.
Carry me, moldy trucks,
to the paradise of the onion and blonde plaits
where I can bathe my eyes
in the vision of a world bejeweled by dew.

Weigh, weigh fish and lettuce:
weigh the whole moon,
weigh sweetened hearts by the pound,
tears by the liter,
weigh a salad of dreams,
pull all the love of the world from the trucks,
all that pure cargo
prepared through months of labor
and by the fertilizing patience of water.

A stork of oil pecks at the moon,
as shadows devour the last white horses.
I say stork: my mind thinks tin,
while in the window a river sparkles
without being able to enter.

Todas las plumas
de la luna y la cigüeña
caben en la funda de la nube
durante varios días.
Después las plumas caen y es el invierno.

Listo para el asador
se vende el invierno ya desplumado.
El vino del crepúsculo en las remolachas
alarma la inocencia de la lechuga
 hermana mayor de la rosa.
Oh repollo, linaje del suelo
bendecido por la lluvia:
las cabezas de la familia real conducida en la carreta
al último suplicio
caerán en el saco.

Camiones, grandes cofres de lona
repletos de viento
 llevadme a la comarca escondida
donde nunca mueren las hojas
junto al agua que refleja un rostro inocente
entre legumbres redondas como la luna
¡oh comarca del rocío
fuera de las rutas que conducen
a la frontera final guardada por los cuervos!

For several days
all the feathers
of the moon and stork
slip into an envelope of clouds.
Later, feathers fall and it's winter.

Ready for the spit, already plucked,
winter is sold.
A wine of twilight in the beets
alarms the innocence of the lettuce,
older spinster sister of the rose.
Oh, cabbage! lineage of soil
blessed by rain:
heads of the royal family carried by cart
to a final punishment,
they will fall into the sack.

Trucks, huge coffers of canvas
filled by wind:
carry me to the hidden region
where leaves never die,
next to the water that reflects an innocent face,
among vegetables round like the moon.
Oh, region of morning dew,
far away from the roads that lead
to a final frontier guarded by ravens!

1966

Cuaderno del Paracaidista

Sólo encontré dos pájaros y el viento,
las nubes con sus mapas enrollados
y unas flores de humo que se abrian buscándome
durante el vertical viaje celeste.

Porque vengo del cielo
como en las profecías y en los himnos,
emisario de lo alto, con mi uniforme de hojas,
mi provisión de vidas y de muertes.

Del cielo voy bajando como el día.
Humedezco los párpados
de aquellos que me esperan: he seguido
la ruta de la luz y de la lluvia.

Buen arbusto, protéjeme.
Dile, tierra, a tu surco mojado que me acoja
y a ese tronco caído
que me enseñe el color, la forma inerte.

¡Aquí estoy, campesinos europeos!
Vengo en nombre del pan, de las madres del mundo,
de toda la blancura degollada:
la garza, la azucena, el cordero, la nieve.

Fortalecen mi brazo ciudades en escombros,
familias mutiladas, dispersas por la tierra,
niños y campos rubios viviendo, desde hace años,
siglos de noche y sangre.

CENTURY OF THE DEATH OF THE ROSE

The Parachutist's Notebook

I encountered only two birds and wind,
clouds with their scrolled maps,
and some flowers of smoke that opened looking for me
during the vertical drop through the sky.

I come from the sky,
just as in prophecies and hymns,
an emissary from the heights, wearing a uniform of leaves,
with my inventory of living and dead.

I come down like day from the sky.
I moisten the eyelids
of those who wait for me: I followed
the path of light and rain.

Good shrub, protect me.
Earth, tell your damp furrows to cushion me,
tell this fallen tree
to teach me color, inert form.

Peasants of Europe, here I am!
I come in the name of bread, of the mothers of the world,
of all this decapitated whiteness:
the heron, the lily, the lamb, and snow.

My arm is strengthened by ruined cities,
mutilated families scattered over the earth,
living children and blonde fields
that have endured centuries of night and blood.

Campesinos del mundo: he bajado del cielo
 como una blanca umbela o medusa del aire.
Traigo ocultos relámpagos o provisión de muertes,
pero traigo también las cosechas futuras.

Traigo la mies tranquila sin soldados,
las ventanas con luz otra vez, persiguiendo
la noche para siempre derrotada.
Yo soy el nuevo ángel de este siglo.

Ciudadano del aire y de las nubes,
poseo sin embargo una sangre terrestre
que conoce el camino que entra a cada morada,
el camino que fluye debajo de los carros,

las aguas que pretenden ser las mismas
que ya pasaron antes,
la tierra de animales y legumbres con lágrimas
donde voy a encender el día con mis manos.

Peasants of the world: I come down from the sky
like a white umbrella or jellyfish of the air.
I bring hidden lightning, a reservoir of death,
but I also bring the future harvests.

I bring tranquil wheat without soldiers,
windows filled with light again,
pursuing forever the defeated night.
I am the new angel of this century.

A citizen of the air and clouds,
I still, however, possess a terrestrial blood
that knows the paths to each dwelling,
the roads that flow beneath wagons,

waters that pretend to be the same,
that have passed before,
this earth of tearful animals and vegetables
where I will ignite the day with my hands.

                                        1944

Dibujo del Hombre

El mundo está cubierto de cunas
que cantan en la noche.

El hombre vive amontonando cubos de piedra
para las casas de los futuros hombres.

Agobiado de climas,
orientado entre torres, chimeneas y antenas,
viajero cada día en su ciudad,
náufrago desde las cinco
entre una vegetación eléctrica de avisos.

Amaestrador de máquinas,
habitante de los rascacielos.
Estás al norte y al sur, al este y al oeste:
hombre blanco, hombre amarillo, hombre negro.

Florecen en sus manos
itinerarios de trenes y de barcos.
Se suman en sus ojos
las mañanas nutridas de periódicos.

El ferrocarril cepilla la tierra
estirando virutas de paisajes
y el avión se levanta contra la geografía
guiado por el hombre de manos perfectas.

El hombre grita
en México y Berlín, en Moscú y Buenos Aires
y sus radiogramas cubren el planeta.

CENTURY OF THE DEATH OF THE ROSE

Portrait of Man

The world is covered with cradles
that sing in the night.

Man lives accumulating blocks of stone
for the houses of the future man.

Weighed down by climates,
oriented among towers, chimneys and antennae,
a traveler each day in his city,
shipwrecked by five o'clock
among an electric vegetation of advertisements.

Master of machines,
inhabitant of skyscrapers.
You are in the North, South, East and West:
white man, yellow man, black man.

In his hands bloom
itineraries of boats and trains.
Nourished by newspapers
mornings are summed up in his eyes.

The railroad plows through the earth,
turning up shavings of landscapes;
and piloted by the man with perfect hands
the airplane rises against the geography.

Man shouts
in Mexico and Berlin, in Moscow and Buenos Aires
as his telegrams cover the planet.

Este es el paisaje de nuestra noche:
La ciudad se ciñe su cinturón de trenes,
cuernos de caracol sacan los proyectores
y desciende un avión, náufrago celeste.

Y se levanta el Hombre, inventor del futuro,
circundado de máquinas,
carteles de Lenín, planos de Nueva York
y panoramas del mundo.

This is the landscape of our night:
the city girds on its belt of trains,
as searchlights extend their snail's antenna
and an airplane, a celestial shipwreck, descends.

Man, inventor of the future, arises
surrounded by machines,
posters of Lenin, street plans of New York
and panoramas of the world.

1935

Los Terrícolas

Os digo: nuestro siglo es fabuloso.
Crepúsculo del Hombre
sitiado por millares de terrícolas
sin ojos para ver nubes o flores,
sólo nutridos de oro,
incapaces de oír la música del mundo,
aprendices o larvas del Autómata próximo.

Terrícolas que entierran las estatuas,
emparedan los libros
echan al mar las llaves del planeta,
desconocen el lirio,
todo ponen en venta, hasta el claro de luna,
proclaman el mundial degüello de los cisnes
como materia prima para una nueva industria.

Terrícolas iguales en su gesto y ropaje
y por dentro vacíos,
negadores del sol, seres de sombra
falanges del bostezo y del olvido,
sublevación inmensa
contra el Hombre y su mundo de amor y maravilla
para instaurar el reino de las Palabras Huecas.

El reino de los cielos con máquinas volantes,
el reino de las músicas mecánicas
y las Casas Idénticas
—desmesuradas tumbas con pisos y ventanas—
el Reino Sordomudo
obediente a señales y cifras luminosas,

THE TERRESTRIANS

I tell you: ours is a fabulous century,
Twilight of Man,
beseiged by thousands of terrestrians
too blind to see clouds or flowers,
nourished only on gold,
incapable of hearing the world's music,
apprentices or larvae to the coming Age of the Automaton.

Terrestrians who bury statues
lock away books,
throw keys of the planet into the sea;
have never heard of lilies,
will sell anything, even moonlight,
proclaim a worldwide cutting of swan's throats
to provide the basic material for a new industry.

Terrestrians, all dressing and acting the same
and yet empty inside,
these deniers of sunlight, shadow beings,
phalanxes of yawns and oblivion
lead an immense uprising
against Man and his world of love and marvels
to restore the Kingdom of Empty Words.

A kingdom of skies filled with flying machines,
a kingdom of mechanical music
and Identical Houses
—enormous tombs with floors and windows—
the Kingdom of the Deaf and Dumb,
obedient to signs and luminous numbers,

JORGE CARRERA ANDRADE

palpitantes avispas de los muros.

No existen manantiales
en la Ciudad Terrícola.
En moradas de vidrio
la sed eterna habita.
La sed huye en torrentes de automóviles
hacia constelaciones de neón y regresa
en su ronda mortal de insectos de colores.

¡Oh siglo fabuloso!
El planeta contempla la agonía
de los últimos hombres
acosados sin fin por los terrícolas
dinámicos, idénticos
que avanzan sepultando los cuadros y los libros,
fortaleza final de los humanos sueños.

wasps palpitating in the walls.

There are no springs
in the Terrestrial City.
Eternal thirst
lives in glass dwellings.
Thirst flees in torrents of automobiles
toward neon constellations, and returns
in its mortal night patrol of colored insects.

Oh, fabulous century!
The planet contemplates the agony
of the last men
endlessly pursued by those
identical and dynamic Terrestrians,
that move forward burying paintings and books,
the last fortresses of human dreams.

1955

Invocación al Aire

Te invoco dios del aire,
el del traje de vidrio
y la corona azul de plumería
ahora que me siento profundamente urbano
tan repleto de gente como una plaza pública.

Te invoco dios del aire,
el de alas transparentes.
Yo súbdito de un reino anterior a la rueda,
me siento atravesado por miles de automóviles
como una pista gris en el crepúsculo.

Tú, nutrido de espacio y de suspiros,
dios de plumas azules,
morador solitario de la altura,
cédeme una parcela de tu reino.
Dentro de mí la multitud habita
y ya no tengo sitio para vivir conmigo.

INVOCATION TO THE AIR

God of air,
in your costume of glass
and crown of blue feathers,
I invoke you now that I feel profoundly urban,
as full of people as a public square.

God of air, with transparent wings,
as citizen of an era that preceded the wheel,
I invoke you now that I am run over
by thousands of cars,
like a gray highway in the twilight.

Nourished by space and sighs,
god of blue feathers,
solitary dweller in the heights
relinquish to me a small bit of your kingdom.
The multitude lives within me,
and I have no room left to live with myself.

1966

Imagen Entera

De pronto me vi
imagen entera
con un gesto aprendido
a través de los años.
Yo era hombre de cristal
que reflejaba el mundo
sin nada retener.
Me vi distinto
a las otras imágenes
de mí mismo
vivas en el espejo:
más sombra en mi cabeza
a mis pies más abismo,
en mi interior más selva,
inconsciencia de planta
obediente a la brisa
junco de soledad
ya no pensante
—¡soledad terrenal
única compañía!—.
Me vi en fugaz reflejo
mirando desde afuera
al ser que vive dentro
recluso enmascarado
en su ambulante encierro.

The Whole Image

Suddenly I saw the whole
image of myself,
with a gesture learned
through the years.
I was a man of crystal
who reflected the world
and held nothing back.
I saw myself distinct
from other images
of myself
alive in the mirror:
more shadow on my head,
more abyss at my feet,
more forest in my interior,
unconsciousness of a plant
obedient to the breeze,
a reed of solitude
that no longer thinks
—earthly solitude
my only company!—
I saw myself in a fleeting reflection,
looking from outside
at the self who lives within,
a masked recluse
in his wandering prison.

1966

Estación Penúltima

A mi vuelta de exóticos países
después de cada viaje
mis lágrimas derramo como Ulises.

En su gran recipiente de cristal la ventana
me ofrece el mundo entero
desde el cielo oriental de porcelana

hasta el trigal cristiano panadero
las lanzas del maíz americano
y el campo universal con su sendero.

Inútil viaje. Vuelta inoportuna:
suspiro como Ulises
por la Ítaca celeste de la luna.

The Last Station

After each voyage,
I weep like Ulysses
arriving home from exotic countries.

The window offers me a whole wide world
through its great crystal portal,
from the sky of oriental porcelain,

to wheat fields of the Christian baker,
to lances of American corn,
and the universal field with its footpath.

A useless voyage. A premature return:
I sigh, like Ulysses,
for the celestial Ithaca of the moon.

1966

Viaje de Regreso

Mi vida fue una geografía
que repasé una y otra vez,
libro de mapas o de sueños.
En América desperté.

¿Soñé acaso pueblos y ríos?
¿No era verdad tanto país?
¿Hay tres escalas en mi viaje:
soñar, despertar y morir?

Me había dormido entre estatuas
y me hallé solo al despertar.
¿Dónde están las sombras amables?
¿Amé y fui amado de verdad?

Una geografía de sueño,
una historia de magia fue.
Sé de memoria islas y rostros
vistos o soñados tal vez.

Sobre el botín del universo
— fruta, mujer, inmensidad —
se echaron todos mis sentidos
como ebrios corsarios del mar.

En un puerto, joven desnuda,
forma cabal, por fin te hallé:
en tu agua grande, estremecida,
yo saciaba mi humana sed.

The Return Journey

My life was a geography
I surveyed over and over again,
a book of maps or dreams.
In America I awoke.

Did I dream perhaps of rivers and towns?
Was there nothing real about these countries?
Are there three steps in my journey:
dreaming, waking, and dying?

I've fallen asleep among statues
and upon waking found myself alone.
Where are the benevolent shadows?
Did I love and in truth was I loved?

It was a geography of dream,
a magical history.
I know by memory the islands and faces
seen or, perhaps, dreamed.

Upon the spoils of the universe
— fruit, woman, the immensity —
fell all of my senses,
like drunken pirates of the sea.

At last I found you in harbor,
naked girl, perfectly shaped:
in your great, tremulous water
I quenched my human thirst.

Luego fue la niña de trigo,
fue la doncella vegetal;
mas, siempre, desde cada puerta
me llamaba la Otra eternal.

Desde la nieve a la palmera
la tierra de ciudades vi.
Dios limpiaba allí las ventanas
y nadie quería morir.

Vi la seca tierra del toro
— postrer refugio del azul —
y el país donde erige el pino
su verde obelisco a la luz.

¿Soñé ese rostro sobre el muro,
esa mano sobre mi piel,
ese camino de manzanas
y palomas, soñé, soñé?

¿Las bahías cual rebanadas
de una sandía de cristal
y sus islas como semillas
fueron un sueño y nada más?

¿Ceniza mortal este polvo
que se adhiere aún a mis pies?
¿No fueron puertos sino años
los lugares en donde anclé?

En los más distintos idiomas
sólo aprendí la soledad
y me gradué doctor en sueños.
Vine a América a despertar.

Later came the maiden of wheat,
the vegetal virgin;
but, always, from each door
the eternal Other called me.

From snow to palm tree
I saw cities of the earth
where God had cleaned the windows
and no one wanted to die.

I saw the arid earth of the bull
—last refuge of blue—
and a country where pine trees
raise their green obelisks to the light.

Did I dream this face on the wall,
that hand upon my skin?
This street of apples
and doves, did I dream it all?

The harbor like equal sections
of a crystal watermelon,
and islands like seeds:
was this a dream and nothing more?

Is this dust the mortal ash
that still clings to my feet?
Were they not harbors but years,
those places I anchored in?

Only in the most distinct languages
did I become fluent in solitude
and graduated as a doctor of dreams.
I came to America to awake.

Mas, de nuevo arde en mi garganta
sed de vivir, sed de morir
y humilde doblo la rodilla
sobre esta tierra del maíz.

Tierra de frutas y de tumbas,
propiedad única del sol:
Vengo del mundo—¡oh largo sueño!—
y un mapa se enrolla en mi voz.

But, in my throat burns
the thirst to live, the thirst to die,
and so I humbly bend down
to this earth of maize.

Land of fruit and tombs,
sole property of the sun:
I come from the world—Oh, great dream!—
with a map scrolled in my voice.

1950

Jorge Carrera Andrade— Biographical Sketch And Chronology

Jorge Carrera Andrade was born in Quito, Ecuador, on September 14, 1902. He was the son of Abelardo Carrera Andrade and Carmen Vaca Andrade. He died November 7, 1978. Carrera Andrade was educated at Juan Montalvo Normal Institute and Mejía National Institute.

Memberships

Asociación General Universitaria Ibero-Americana of Barcelona (Secretary, 1932)
Verband Latein Amerikanischer Studenten von Berlin
Grupo "América," Quito
Sociedad Jurídico-Literaria
Sociedad de Estudios Hispanoamericanistas
Sociedad "Amigos de Montalvo"
Club de Trabajadores Intelectuales
Casa de la Cultura Ecuatoriana, Quito
California Writers Club, San Francisco
Associazione Internazionale di Poesia, Rome
PEN, New York
Academia Ecuatoriana de la Lengua

Chronology

1902   Born September 14 in Quito.
1921   Graduates from el Instituto Nacional Mejia.
1922   Publishes first book of poetry, *Estanque inefable*.
1923   Helps to organize Ecuadorian Socialist Party.
1927   Publishes *La Guirnalda del Silencio*
1927-28   Secretary-general of the Ecuadorian Socialist Party.
1928   Statistician of the Bureau of Studies (Dirección de Estudios); travels to Europe and meets Gabriela Mistral and César

Vallejo.

1929   Named Chancellor of Ecuadorian Consulate in Marseilles, France.

1930   Publishes *Boletines de mar y tierra* in Barcelona.

1933   Secretary of Ecuadorian Senate; Professor, Mejía National Institute, Quito.

1934   Consul in Paita, Perú.

1934   Consul in Le Havre, France.

1935   Marries Paulette Colin Lebas; publishes *Rol de la manzana* and *El tiempo manual* in Spain.

1937   Birth of son, Juan Cristobal.

1938-40   Consul General in Yokohama, Japan; publishes *País secreto* in Tokyo; publishes *Antologia poetica, 1922-1939* in Quito.

1940-44   Consul General in San Francisco, California; begins friendship with Pedro Salinas.

1944   Chargé d'affaires in Caracas, Venezuela.

1945   Publishes *Poems of Paul Valery* in Spanish translation in Caracas, Venezuela.

1946   Resigns from diplomatic post to protest President Velasco Ibarra's breach of the Ecuadorian constitution; wife begins divorce proceedings.

1947   Senator of the Republic of Ecuador; named by President Carlos Julio Arosemena Envoy Extraordinaire and Minister Plenipotentiary to Great Britain.

1948   Delegate to the Third General Assembly of the United Nations in Paris.

1949   Delegate to the Fourth Conference of UNESCO.

1950   Returns to Quito and is named Head of the Section for Diplomacy of the Ministry of Foreign Relations; six months later resigns and is named Vice President of Casa de la Cultura, Quito.

1951   Publishes in Quito, *Poesía Francesa Contemporánea*, an anthology of fifty-five French poets in Spanish translation; anthology receives Isle Saint-Louis Prize from French government; *Lugar de origen* appears in Quito. Ministry of Education names Carrera Andrade as Permanent delegate to UNESCO and he returns to Paris. Marries Janina Ruffier des Aimes.

1952   With electoral triumph of Velasco Ibarra, Carrera Andrade resigns position. Begins employment with UNESCO as director of Spanish publications. Birth of daughter, Patricia.

1953   Second edition of *Familia de noche* is published in Paris.

1955   *La tierra siempre verde*, published in Paris.

1958   *Moneda del forastero* in a bilingual edition (Spanish-French) is published in Paris. Leaves job at UNESCO and transfers to New York as member of Ecuadorian delgation to the United Nations.

1959   *Hombre planetario* appears in Bogota; *El camino del sol* appears in Quito.

1960   President Velasco Ibarra names Carrera Andrade ambassador for Special Mission to governments of Chile, Argentina, and Brazil. Participates in successful negotiation of Treaty of Rio de Janeiro.

1961   Named ambassador to Venezuela.

1962   *Mi vida en poemas* published in Caracas.

1963   President Arosemena Monroy is deposed and a military junta is established. Venezuela suspends relations with Ecuador and Carrera Andrade is forced to resign as ambassador.

1964   Named ambassador to France; publishes in Nicaragua a poem and two books: "Floresta de los guacamayos," *Radiografía de la cultura ecuatoriana* and *Interpretaciones de Rúben Dario*.

1965   Publishes in Paris *Crónicas de las Indias*.

1966   The new president of Ecuador, Otto Arosemena, names Carrera Andrade Minister of Foreign Relations.

1967   President Arosemena accepts a denunciation of Carrera Andrade by the political right.

1968   Participates in International Poetry Festival at the Poetry Center in New York City and Festival of Poetry at State

University of New York (SUNY) at Stony Brook.

1969   Named Distinguished Professor at SUNY Stony Brook.

1970   Participates in Festival of International Poetry organized by the Library of Congress in Washington, D.C.; an autobiography, *El volcán y colibrí*, appears in Mexico; bilingual Spanish-French edition of *El libro del destierro* appears in Dakar, South Africa.

1971   Lecture at Harvard; terminates teaching position at SUNY Stony Brook and returns to Paris.

1972   *Jorge Carrera Andrade: Introducción al estudio de su vida y de su obra* by J. Enrique Ojeda appears in Madrid; *Selected Poems*, translated by H. R. Hays published by SUNY Press.

1973   Lectures from Harvard, Stony Brook, and Vassar College collected as *Reflections on Spanish American Poetry* (SUNY Press).

1975   Director of Biblioteca Nacional, Quito. *Obra poetica completa* published in Quito. Academia de la Lengua del Ecuador nominates Carrera Andrade for Nobel Prize in literature. Government of Ecuador awards him "Eugenio Espejo" prize in recognition of his extraordinary literary accomplishments and contributions to Ecuadorian culture.

1978   November 7 Jorge Carrera Andrade dies and is buried in the Cemetery of San Diego, Quito.

Jorge Carrera Andrade: A Partial Bibliography

Prose in English

Carrera Andrade, Jorge, "The New American and His Point of View Toward Poetry," tr. H.R. Hays, *Poetry* (Chicago), LXII, 1943, p. 88–105.

H.R. Hays, "Jorge Carrera Andrade: Magician of Metaphors," *Books Abroad* (Norman, OK), XVII, No. 2, 1943, p. 101–105.

Books in English

To the Oakland Bridge, tr. Eleanor Turnbull, Palo Alto: Stanford University Press, 1941.

Secret Country, tr. Muna Lee, New York: MacMillan, 1946.

The Selected Poems of Jorge Carrera Andrade, tr. H.R. Hays, Albany: SUNY press, 1972.

Reflections on Latin American Literature, tr. Don and Gabriela C. Bliss, Albany: SUNY Press, 1973.

Century of the Death of the Rose: The Selected Poems, tr. Steven Ford Brown, Montgomery: NewSouth Books, 2002.

Books in Spanish

Autobiography

The Volcano and the Hummingbird, Puebla, Mexico: Editorial José M. Cajica Jr., S.A., 1970.

Essays

Latitudes, Quito: Talleres Graficos Nacionales, 1934; Buenos Aires: Editor "Parseo," 1940.

Interpretations of Hispano-America, Quito: Casa de la Cultura Ecuatoriana, 1967.

History (A three-volume history of Ecuador)

Land Always Green, Paris: Ediciones Internacionales, 1955.

Gallery of Mystics and Insurgents, Quito: Casa de la Ecuatoriana, 1959.

The Kingdom of Quito or Street of The Sun, Quito: Casa de la Cultura Ecuatoriana, 1963.

Memoir

Traveller Through Countries and Books, Quito: Casa de la Cultura Ecuatoriana, 1961.

Poetry

Wreath of Silence, Quito: Casa de la Cultura Ecuatoriana, 1926.

Indian Poems, Quito: Editorial Elan, 1928.

Earth and Sea Bulletines (Foreword by Gabriela Mistral), Barcelona: Editorial Cervantes, 1930.

Time Manual, Madrid: Editions Literatura: PEN Coleccion, 1935; French translation by Adolphe de Falgairolle, Paris: Editions Rene Debresse, 1936.

Biography for the Use of Birds, Paris: Cuadernos del Hombre Nuevo, 1937; French translation by Edmond Vandercammen, Brussels: Les Cahiers du Journal des Poetes, 1937.

Anthology of Pierre Reverdy, Tokyo: Editions Asia America, 1939.

Secret Country, Toyko: Editions Asia America, 1940.

Place of Origin, Caracas: Editions Suma, 1944.

Family of Night, Paris: Libreria Espanola de Ediciones, 1953.

Planetary Man, Quito: Editorial Elan, 1963

Poesía última, ed. with introduction, J. Enrique Ojeda, New York: Las Americas Publishing Co., 1968.

BOOKS IN FRENCH

Les armes de la lumière, tr. Fernand Verhesen. Bruxelles, Editions Le Cormier, 1953.

Monnaie de L'etranger, Collection Terres Fortunees, Paris, 1958.

Livre de l'exil precede de Message al Afrique, tr. Rene L. F. Durand. Dakar: Centre de Hautes Etudes Afro-Ibero-Americaines, 1970.

BOOKS IN GERMAN

Poemas / Gedichte. Übertragen von F. Vogelsang. Stuttgart, Klett-Cotta 1980.

About the Editor and Translator

Steven Ford Brown's translations of Angel Gonzalez (Spain), Pablo de Rohka (Chile), Pere Gimferrer (Catalonia), and Ana Maria Fagndo (Spain) have appeared in *The Christian Science Monitor, Harvard Review, The Marlboro Review, Poetry, Quarterly West,* and *Verse.* His books include *Astonishing World: The Selected Poems of Angel Gonzalez, 1956-1986* (Milkweed Editions, 1993), *Invited Guest: An Anthology of Twentieth-Century Southern Poetry* (University of Virginia Press, 2001), *Edible Amazonia: Twenty-One Poems from God's Amazonian Recipe Book,* translations of the poetry of Nicomedes Suarez-Arauz (Bolivia) (Bitter Oleander Press, 2002), and *One More River To Cross: The Selected Poems of John Beecher* (NewSouth Books, 2002). Excerpts from his translation of *Astonishing World* were included in *The Vintage Anthology of Contemporary World Poetry,* edited by J. D. McClatchy (Vintage/Random House, 1996). To support his translation of *Astonishing World* he received a translation grant from the Ministerio de Cultura, Madrid, Spain. The American Association of University Presses and the University Press Books Committee chose *Invited Guest: An Anthology of Twentieth-Century Southern Poetry* as one of the "Best of the Best from the University Presses" for 2001. He lives in Boston.